Testimonials

Don Burrows doesn't miss a thing in this hot new book. It's about HOW TO stand out. This is functional profile methodology and its emphasis on customization and sharing your personal interests is right on in today's world dominated by social media. Don helps you uncover and present accomplishments that make you look like the rock star that you are. There are many great tips here for business people as well.

Mike O'Neil | President, Founder, Trainer, Speaker, Author, LinkedIn Rock Star
Integrated Alliances | www.integratedalliances.com
Phone (303) 683-9600 Office | **(720) 897-8254 Direct**

Author *Rock The World with your Online Presence* LinkedIn Book
LinkedIn www.linkedin.com/in/mikeoneil 27,000+ connections
Twitter @mikeoneildenver 27,000+ followers

Don is a true professional career coach. He knows how to get the candidate thinking like a winner. By using his methodology, it prepares a job seeker to answer tough interview questions and present themselves in the best light, all by focusing on accomplishments. I have found his advice invaluable as I navigated my personal career journey. He is able to breathe confidence into the resume and into the candidate. Following his advice, I refocused my resume, and myself, on accomplishments, saying "why", and "so what" to provide eloquent, complete talking points for phone and face-to-face interviews, showing my true value to any employer.

Rachel Braynin | Director, Global Support, ChannelAdvisors

As a Human resources professional, I have seen many, many resumes. There are about four or five common formats that, in time, become variations on a main theme: here's where I worked; when I worked; what I was responsible for.

You would think I would have developed a sense of what would be the "perfect resume".

Instead, like the hand that does a lot of manual labor, I developed a callous, albeit a mental one. I became increasingly unable to get a "feel" for the candidates and likely missed some good ones.

Fortunately, when I was looking for work, I had an opportunity to use Don Burrows' approach to writing a Functional Resume. The effect was twofold. I got more interviews than I had with a traditionally formatted résumé – and yes, I got the job I wanted.

But even more important to me professionally, I got to be a better HR professional … I learned what it takes to make résumés do what a résumé should do … get you in front of the person who will make the hiring decision.

Don's intelligent, insightful approach will help your résumé stand out and get you that interview.

JonScott Williams | Organization Development / Human Resources Consultant

Don participated in a multi-state downsizing event that impacted employees who had been with our company for 20+ years. An effort was made to assist these employees in preparing to land new jobs and that is where Don's talents came into play. Without much more than a few marching orders and a map of the east coast Don set off to meet affected individuals and help them prepare a resume, practice interviewing techniques, and develop a job search strategy. His assistance was instrumental in a successful downsizing that resulted in no adverse action against the company. And, he truly made a measurable difference for each of the individuals to which he devoted his time and talent.

Ann Coplin | VP Human Resources, Retired

Wow! The information in this book is PRICELESS. I took your advice and within a day I was getting interest from employers. Don is the real deal and if you don't get this book you will be unemployed for a long time.

Eric Castaneda | Author *Action Mentality: How to Fulfill Your Dream*
www.ericcastaneda.com

Don, I really have to thank you for getting me in touch with Lowe's and their garden department. I've never worked in the retail world before and was concerned if I could handle it but it was really enjoyable. I even got a customer commendation the first week I was there – WOW!

Thank you for opening up a whole new world for me.

Connie Murry | Snohomish, WA

"If you want to get back to work, your resume has to STAND OUT from your competition. You can't do that if you use the same generic, one-size-fits-all resume when applying for SPECIFIC positions. In Résumés That Resume Careers, you'll learn how easy it is to customize your resume according to the requirements of each job you apply for, and present yourself as the unique solution to that company's needs. Read and apply this book to your job search and you will soar!

Patrick Snow | International Best-Selling Author of *Creating Your Own Destiny*

Résumés That Resume Careers

3 Steps to
Getting Back to Work Using
Functional Résumés

Don Burrows
PO Box 1800
Marysville, WA 98270
www.ResumesThatResumeCareers.com
800.597.9972

Résumés that Resume Careers – Three Steps to Getting Back to Work Using Functional Résumés

Address inquiries to:

Donald M. Burrows
C/O Acorn Consulting Inc.
PO Box 1800
Marysville, WA 98270
Telephone: 800.597.9972
www.ResumesThatResumeCareers.com or *www.OneInAMillionResumes.com*

ISBN: 978-0-615-35039-4
Publisher: Aviva Publications, Lake Placid, NY *www.avivapubs.com*
Consultant Editor: Richard Geasey *www.PracticalLocalSearch.com/*
Consultant Editor: Shannon Evans *www.SmallBusinessMarketingToolkits.com*
Associate Editor: Jennifer Haga
Guest Editor: Christopher Burrows
Cover Design: Matthew Mikulsky *www.ChatterCreative.com*
Author Photo: Dennis Wright *www.DWWPhotographicImages.com*

Printed in the United States of America

First Edition

2 4 6 8

a life can change in a tenth of
a second
or sometimes it can take
70
years.

Charles Bukowski
you tell me what it means
The Flash of Lightening Behind the Mountain

Dedication

I dedicate this book to President Barack Obama.

This book came about because of your call for citizens to volunteer our skills to help each other out of this recession.

In response, I created and conducted a series of free public workshops to teach people how to write a more effective résumé – a *functional* résumé.

Participant response was gratifying. Using the format I taught them, their phones finally began to ring with invitations for interviews.

Thank you for being my inspiration to give back to my community and to help people get back to work.

I believe you are a man of vision, integrity and courage, all of which you will need to lead us out of the almost insurmountable mess you inherited.

You have both my respect and my support.

Thank you.

Don Burrows, Marysville, WA

My Thanks...

To **Shannon Evans**, my friend and colleague, for suggesting I convert the download of my functional résumé-writing workshop into a print-on-demand book, and then guiding me through the process

To **Richard Geasey**, Shannon's business partner and my new friend, for his part in the POD process and applying his search engine optimization expertise to my website

To **Jennifer Haga**, my daughter, for taking what I taught her about writing functional résumés to a completely new level and then sharing her ideas with me

To **Chris Burrows**, my son, for letting me help him with his technical résumé, then improving on what we created, and sharing his format with me

To **Rachel Braynin**, my entrepreneurial friend who encourages wide distribution of this book and its companion workshop

To **JonScott Williams**, my wise counselor and articulate supporter of this book and of Mr. Obama

To **Alisha Sylvester**, for using her sales abilities to help me market the book

Finally, to **Karin Burrows**, my wife, who took care of me while I took care of the book.

Testimonials 3

Dedication.. 11

My Thanks… 12

Preface 17

Why I Have Earned the Right to Advise You 19

Thoughts about Unemployment, Dating, Reverse-Chronological and Functional Résumés 21

Introduction to the Process: Overview and Explanation 23

We Begin with This Basic Premise: 25

My Twelve Predictions for Your Job Search 26

Elements of a Functional Résumé 29

Step 1: Customize Your Objective Each Time You Submit Your Résumé.. 31

    Exercise: Writing Objectives 37

Step 2: Create and Draw from a Data Bank of your "Representative Professional Accomplishments" to customize your résumé each time you submit it. 39

    Converting "Activities" Into "Accomplishments" 43

    "So What?" 44

    Power Words 46

    Exercise: Identifying Powerful Words that Describe You 48

    Introduction to Exercise: Writing your Accomplishments 48

    Exercise: Writing Your Accomplishments Essays 51

    Welcome Back! 55

    Welcome Back, *Again* 57

    Exercise: The Essence of Your Accomplishments 57

    Your Accomplishments Data Bank 58

Organizing Your Accomplishments: Subcategories and Key Words.. 60

Recapping Accomplishments 61

STEP 3: Create and draw from a Data Bank of your "Special Skills and Abilities" to customize your résumé each time you submit it. 63

Special Skills and Abilities 63

More About What You Bring to the "World of Work" 65

How to Identify Your Special Skills and Abilities 68

Exercise: Identifying Your Transferrable Skills (Adapted from *What Color Is Your Parachute?* by Richard Bolles/2001 ed. www.JobHuntersBible.com) 70

Exercise: Identifying Your MOTIVATED SKILLS 75

Special Skills and Abilities Data Bank 76

Recapping Special Skills and Abilities 77

Other Categories of Your Résumé 77

Narrative Format: 81

Introduction to Selectivity Exercise: Using Your Data Banks 81

Exercise: Selectivity / Using Your Data Banks 83

Data Bank: Special Skills and Abilities 86

Data Bank: Representative Professional Accomplishments 88

Your Fill-In Practice Résumé 99

Exercise Comments 113

Two Additional Formats 115

One-Page + Addendum Format 115

Technical + Narrative Format 133

Recapping Sample Functional Résumés 142

Bonus Section 143

    Stand Out! 143

    •   Targeted Cover Letters 143

    •   Exploratory Cover Letters 143

    •   Job Search Strategies 143

    •   Four Magic Sentences 143

    Using Your New Résumé in Ways that Make You
    Stand Out 145

    Introduction to Cover Letters 145

    Elements of Targeted Cover Letters............................. 147

    Strategy for Exploratory Letters for Mass Mailing 151

    Be Bold: The Spaghetti or the Meatball? 152

    Four Magic Sentences.. 161

In Closing... 162

Epilogue... 163

Preface

Today is February 2, 2010.

As I write these words, it is 3:06 pm Pacific time and 6:06 pm in New York. Wall Street has closed.

According to CNN's lead business story just now, the Dow posted its second triple digit gain in two days and closed at 10,296.

On this date last year, the Dow closed at 7,796.

Over the last year, the Dow has improved 2,500 points.

Clearly the economy is improving for some people. Are you among them?

If you are reading this book, I suspect your economic situation has not improved quite as well as the Dow's.

My purpose in writing this book is to give you a tool that you can use to improve your own economic situation.

You don't know me, but if you did, you'd know I'm not into quick fixes. I am into common sense and straight talk.

If you have your résumé handy, please get it and let's take a look at the content.

Ask yourself if your résumé is filled with "activities," for example*:*

"Met with employees and explained company benefits."

How about this example of "responsibilities"?

"Responsible for writing and maintaining security and emergency evacuation plan."

Or what about "job duties"? Like this, for example:

"Analyzed results of quarterly inventory figures."

Activities, Responsibilities, Job Duties. SO WHAT?? The fact is, i*n today's job market, employers and recruiters do not care about your job duties, your responsibilities or your work activities.*

They care about problems you have faced and fixed. They care about your <u>skills,</u> <u>abilities</u> and <u>accomplishments</u> that are relevant to their requirements.

PLEASE: Stop using a generic, one-size-fits-all résumé to apply for various positions, each of which is unique and different.

INSTEAD, customize your <u>OBJECTIVE</u>, <u>SPECIAL SKILLS AND ABILITIES</u> and <u>REPRESENTATIVE PROFESSIONAL ACCOMPLISHMENTS</u>, based on the requirements for each position for which you apply.

Does that make sense?

I hope so. If you want to learn to present yourself as *One-In-A-Million*, rather than *one-of-a- million*, let's get to work and get you back to work.

Don Burrows

Why I Have Earned the Right to Advise You

Simply put, my clients credit my functional résumés with getting them more calls, sooner, for interviews than when they used traditional reverse-chronological résumés.

Writing functional résumés has been an avocation for over 30 years. I have written hundreds of them, many for free for people who have suddenly found themselves laid off, without funds and in desperate need of an effective résumé. Others I have written for money, between $1,500 and $2,000 per résumé, in Spanish and English.

When the recession hit and President Obama urged us to volunteer in some way to help others, I created and offered a series of free two-hour workshops to teach others how to write their own functional résumés. The workshops were successful and participants encouraged me to create a website to share the course.

My professional Human Resources management experience spans over 30 years. I have recruited, hired and fired employees from entry to executive levels throughout the United States, Latin America, Europe, Australia, New Zealand and the Asia-Pacific Rim.

In my corporate and consulting careers, I have worked in these industries: hospitality, metal-cutting, financial services, agri-business, transportation, global accounting, chemical manufacturing, and concrete production. All of my corporate positions included recruiting, outplacement, candidate assessment, and job search counseling.

When I evaluated and screened résumés, I *always* called those people who told me what they had ACCOMPLISHED, what problems they had faced and fixed. I called those who simply listed job duties and activities only when I had no one else in the pipeline.

Here's something to keep in mind: based on the accomplishments a candidate presented, it was not uncommon for me to interview them for one position, only to end up considering and then hiring them for a higher-level position. Often these were positions for which I was having difficulty finding qualified candidates.

I did this any number of times over my career. Moreover, because I used a functional résumé when I was in the job market, the same thing happened to me when I was hired for my last corporate job; I applied for one position and was hired for another I did not know existed!

Bottom line: *HR's responsibility is to fill jobs with candidates who meet as many of the hiring qualifications as possible. They do that by screening out as many applicants as possible.*

Knowing that fact, doesn't it make a whole lot of sense to customize your résumé for each position so that you present yourself as a match for their qualifications?

In my experience, people who shotgun their résumés doom themselves to a very long job search. After months of no recruiters calling, a silent telephone gets pretty depressing, doesn't it?

Let's make your phone ring.

Thoughts about Unemployment, Dating, Reverse-Chronological and Functional Résumés

I live in the Great Northwest, just north of Seattle.

Today is April 3, 2010 and late this morning I perked up when the voice on the radio said something about "unemployment." On a whim, I Googled the unemployment rates for the states in my region. According to the US Bureau of Labor Statistics, the rates as of February, 2010 were:

Washington: 9.5 percent
Oregon: 10.5 percent
Alaska: 8.5 percent
Idaho: 9.5 percent

In Seattle, the rate was 9.7 percent. Nationwide, our unemployment rate was 10 percent.

As of March, 2010, the Bureau of Labor Statistics reported 15 million people nationwide were unemployed.

Staggering.

~~~

To help people get back to work, I told you I recently offered a series of workshops on how to write a **functional résumé**.

One of the participants, a young engineer in his late twenties, brought his **reverse-chronological résumé** with him and after class told me he had just submitted it to a boat-building firm for a mechanical design engineer position. He told me that he had been on the market for six months and had submitted the very same résumé, absolutely unchanged, to five other companies in three different industries for several types of mechanical and manufacturing engineering positions.

Over the last six months, he had received no calls, was getting worried, and maybe worst of all, since he was without funds, his social life was just as dead as his career.

Focusing on what apparently mattered most, I invited him to think about his social life and asked if he approached each of the women he dated in the exact same way – same words, same little gifts, same clothes, same places for all dates.

"No way, man. Each woman was different, so my approach was different too," he said.

A pause… and the light went on. He got it. The women, the companies, the jobs, the approaches – all different.

He realized that as long as he kept sending the exact SAME résumé to DIFFERENT companies for DIFFERENT positions, he would likely be out of work for a very long time.

To stand out, he realized he needed to relate his previous accomplishments to an employer's present needs, and present himself as the ideal candidate – the solution to their needs.

Now, please extend that realization nationwide. How long do you think it would take for the economy to get back on its feet as companies filled jobs faster and more people got back to work?

Introduction to the Process: Overview and Explanation

Hello! I am glad you are finally here!

The sooner we get started, the sooner an interviewer can call you.

As you proceed through the course, please have a pad of paper handy to jot down sudden thoughts.

You are about to learn a unique process. Once you have mastered it, you will be able to present yourself as a uniquely qualified candidate for any job for which your experience supports your application.

However, like so many things that are unique and special, effort is required before success can occur.

Let's be clear: to create a résumé that will stand out from your job search competitors, you must take these three critical steps, *each time you submit your résumé for consideration.*

STEP 1: Customize your OBJECTIVE. Do this each time you submit your résumé

STEP 2: Use only your most relevant REPRESENTATIVE PROFESSIONAL ACCOMPLISHMENTS. Do this to customize your résumé to meet the experience requirements of each job each time you submit it

STEP 3: Use only your most relevant SPECIAL SKILLS AND ABILITIES. Do this to customize your résumé to meet the skills requirements of each job each time you submit it.
We are going to take the steps in sequence. By the time we are done, I believe you will agree that tailoring your

functional résumé to present yourself as a uniquely-qualified candidate really is as easy as 1 – 2 – 3.

After having completed all three steps, I will introduce you to three types of functional résumés: **the Narrative, the One-Page + Addendum,** and **the Technical + Narrative.** In what I believe will be a thought-provoking exercise, you will have an opportunity to work with an actual Narrative format résumé.

The final section of the course is a *bonus section*. Once you have a brand new and unique résumé, I would prefer you do not waste it using the same old tired, commonplace job search strategies.

In the bonus section, I'll show you how to create a straightforward, targeted cover letter that will enable you to present yourself as the best possible ideal match for the job, in a manner that complements your new résumé.

I will also share job search strategies to help you come to the attention of decision-makers – strategies that have paid off big for me and for clients.

And I'll close with some words for my cover letters that I found to be almost magical in their effectiveness.

Let's get to it.

We Begin with This Basic Premise:

The purpose of your résumé is to get a recruiter to call YOU for an interview.

Until you get called for an interview, beyond the fact that you remain unemployed, nothing much happens.

Meatball or Spaghetti?

Please look only at the spaghetti. Does any single strand stand out from all the others? No, of course not. You could pick any one; they all look alike.

That's how it is with a pile of reverse-chronological résumés on a recruiter's desk: like spaghetti on a plate, all the résumés look alike.

When you use a résumé that does not stand out from the rest, your chances of being called for an interview are slim.

Now, please consider **the meatball**.

That meatball is part of the pile of spaghetti on the plate, but it stands out.

And it's the same for a functional résumé. IT STANDS OUT.

If you want your telephone to ring with a recruiter on the other end calling YOU for an interview, your résumé needs to **stand out** from the competition.

So really, it's up to you.

The prize is an interview and possibly a job offer.

Is it worth the effort to learn how to create a unique functional résumé so **you stand out** *like the meatball*, or are you satisfied with the results you are getting?

Asked another way, could it be that recruiters are not calling you because you are using the same generic reverse-chronological and look just like everyone else?

If your résumé looks like the rest of the spaghetti résumés in the stack of paper on a recruiter's desk, I'd say that might be a problem.

My Twelve Predictions for Your Job Search

If you are still unconvinced that a functional résumé is the way to go, let me make the case this way:

I predict your job search will be long, frustrating and disappointing if your current résumé:

1. Looks like everyone else's résumé. If it does, what would make a recruiter pick your résumé out of an eight-inch pile of fifty reverse-chronological résumés? Not much.

2. Simply lists your job duties and activities. Pretend for a moment that you are the recruiter or hiring manager: As you are thinking about the work problems the new-hire will be expected to fix, you are evaluating two résumés side-by-side. One lists the applicant's job duties and activities; the other presents the applicant's accomplishments - the problems that person has faced and fixed -- and the problems they have fixed are similar to the ones you need fixed. As they say in the movie, "Who You Gonna Call?"

3. *Does not present your ACCOMPLISHMENTS or the successful PROJECTS in a compelling, straightforward, meaningful manner.* There is no question which résumé will be read more closely and which will be quickly skimmed and tossed into the TBNT (Thanks-But-No-Thanks) pile. You absolutely **must** get clear on what you have accomplished, select the accomplishments most relevant to the position for which you are applying, and then tell the recruiter about them.

4. *Focuses on what you want, not on what you can do for the company.* Companies are recruiting to fill a specific need THEY have; they are not a socially-motivated organization there to satisfy your needs. Tell them what you have done for other companies and what you will do for them, not what you want them to do for you.

5. *Shrieks of desperation with an OBJECTIVE that suggests, "I'll do anything."* Referring back to the previous point, unless it is a company's mission to provide employment to people in difficulty, employers do not seek to hire desperate people.

6. *Is boring and fails to catch and hold the recruiter's attention.* When I was a recruiter, it was not unusual for me to go through a foot of résumés in a day, and more at home after dinner. Nothing has eased up. You have about the first ¾ of page one (maybe seven seconds) to catch the attention of a tired and overworked recruiter. If you want to be the one they call, give them quality information that is of interest and matches their needs.

7. *Reads like assembly instructions for a desk.* Most people don't enjoy reading product assembly instructions. YOU are the product. You need to tell the recruiter why you are worth their investment – what <u>benefits</u> will they get when they "buy" you. Contrast that thought with the last time you read the assembly instructions for your child's bicycle.

8. *Is generic, not customized for each position.* You know how you feel when you get a mass-mailing letter addressed to "Dear Sir or Madam?" It generally hits the trash. The same applies when you are applying for a position. Don't be lazy. Personalize your cover letter and customize your résumé for every single position for which you apply. More about that in the Bonus Section.

9. *Forces the recruiter to figure out what you are applying for.* Recruiters are not mind readers. <u>Tell the recruiter</u> what position you are applying for, and then make certain your cover letter and résumé prove you are qualified. This is the time to focus like a laser, not blindly spray like a garden hose. Lasers cut to the chase; water from the hose evaporates.

10. *Calls the reader's attention to your inconsistent work history by presenting it prominently on the first page.* How many employers do you think will jump at the chance to hire someone who has built their career bouncing from job to job to job?

The correct answer is NONE. No employer wants to go to the time and expense of being just another stepping stone and have to go to the time and expense of recruiting and training all over again.

Impressive and relevant accomplishments that are effectively presented can often compensate of an inconsistent work history, so that the recruiter will at least call you and do a phone interview.

11. Raises more questions than it answers. The content of your résumé may cause a ripple of interest, but if your words are unclear and raise more questions than answers, it's very likely the recruiter will decide to pass you by and look elsewhere. You may be qualified, but filling in all the holes, sorting through all the inconsistencies, and getting answers to all of their questions can feel like more trouble than it's worth.

12. Buries relevant information about your skills, abilities and experiences so deep within the résumé that the recruiter never gets to it because of any of the preceding eleven items.

Elements of a Functional Résumé

♦※ Whenever you see one of these -- ♦※ -- please sit up straight and pay attention.

What follows immediately afterward will be critical to your success as you create your functional résumés.

♦※ When I was a recruiter screening résumés, applicants had the first ¾ of the first page to hook my interest. (I know I am repeating myself, but it is critically important.) If they did, it did not matter how many pages were in the résumé. So long as the content was interesting and relevant to a job I needed to fill, I read every word on every page. If the content was boring or irrelevant to my open positions, TBNT. Don't forget: the first ¾ of the first page.

♦※ *Remember, think "MEATBALL," not "spaghetti."* Customizing these three components of your functional résumé, each time you apply for a position, *will enable you to* *create a unique document that will stand out, <u>tailored to each position:</u>*

- *The Objective*
- *Representative Professional Accomplishments*
- *Special Skills and Abilities*

💣 Tailoring these three elements of your résumé, each time, for each position for which you are applying, is absolutely critical. No more using a generic résumé for specific positions.

If that sounds like too much effort, here's a question: how badly do you want to get back to work?

As personal development expert Brian Klemmer says, ***"Judge by results. Often harsh; always fair."***

Step 1: Customize Your <u>Objective</u> Each Time You Submit Your Résumé

Before I show you how to tailor your OBJECTIVE for each position, I want to show you three examples of poor Objectives, and explain why they are ineffective.

Poor Example 1: *"Experienced individual with proven ability in management, supervision, human resource management seeking position that will utilize my diverse background."*

This is a generic, shotgun objective. It lacks focus and requires the recruiter to be a mind reader. What industry? What level of management? Managing what and how many? What else besides Human Resources?

Reading between the lines, it suggests desperation to me. In my experience, companies prefer not to hire people who come across as desperate.

Poor Example 2: *"I am a people-oriented person and I'm seeking a position in which I can develop my supervisory skills while learning about the company."*

I can't help it. The first time I read this, I found myself trying to remember the words to *"Cumbaya."*

Please don't ever forget: the company is not in business to satisfy your wants and needs. YOU are the product, and before they will "buy" YOU, they want to know what YOU have accomplished elsewhere and what you'll do for THEM.

Poor Example 3: *"Any position for which I am qualified."*

For so many reasons, it always saddened me to receive a résumé with this as its Objective.

Early on in my career, when I was still taking baby steps to learn my profession, I felt sorry for people who submitted résumés with that objective. Because my first employer cared about its employees, I thought we could help lost job applicants and called a few for interviews. My staff recruiter told me I was wasting my time, and theirs, because she had learned that people who presented themselves in that manner had nothing *specific* to offer our employer.

A side story: Some years back, I attended a very inspirational presentation called "Homeboy Goes to Harvard." Aimed at at-risk Latino kids, it was given by motivational speaker Richard Santana, (AKA "Mr. Chocolate.")

Among other profoundly insightful observations, Mr. Santana said, *"Stupid people learn from their own mistakes. Smart people learn from the mistakes of others,"* and he proved his point with tragic examples from his childhood in the barrios of Los Angeles. He told us he was not expected to live into his twenties. Please note the title of his presentation.

Returning to Poor Example 3, I did not listen to my recruiter because I thought I knew it all. Over a few months, I interviewed a number of applicants whose résumés had similar *"Any position for which I am qualified"* objectives. Each of those interviews was a waste of everyone's time.

I should have learned from her experience.

Please see **Prediction 5** and be sure your OBJECTIVE is specific.

Proceeding now to our OBJECTIVE …

Let's consider writing the OBJECTIVE as a three-part process.

OBJECTIVE: PART ONE: **The Position**: Let's assume you are an Accounting Manager, or perhaps an Electrical Engineer, or Administrative Assistant or Grass Cutter.

Let's further assume you have seen position announcements, have the necessary qualifications, and want to apply for one of these positions:

1. Finance Manager with Seattle Viaduct Hospital
2. Process Engineer with Seattle Viaduct Hospital
3. Admitting Office Department Secretary with Seattle Viaduct Hospital
4. Grounds Keeper with Seattle Viaduct Hospital

💣* *The first step in creating a customized functional résumé is to make your OBJECTIVE match the position announcement.*

Pretty straight-forward concept.

But so many people ignore it. Perhaps they think it is hokey or not necessary.

Or maybe they ignore it because they are too lazy to modify their résumé because they wrongly think a résumé with a generic OBJECTIVE will be just as effective as one with a specific objective.

Or perhaps they want to keep their options open and so leave it to the recruiter to figure it out.

It is not hokey and it is necessary. And I hope by now I don't need to comment on "lazy" or "generic" or "keeping options open."

💣 Remember, the functional résumé is not about what <u>you</u> need; it is about positioning you as the solution to what the <u>company</u> needs.

So for this exercise, if in real life you are an Accounting Manager, a Quality Engineer, an Administrative Assistant, or a Gardener, please put aside your prior/current position or title and make your OBJECTIVE Finance Manager, Process Engineer, Admitting Office Department Secretary or Grounds Keeper.

You are seeking a new position, not trying to hang on to your old one. Unless you are flexible and prepared to redefine yourself, it will be tough going.

OBJECTIVE: PART TWO: <u>The Required Skills</u>: As you read the position requirements, identify the two or three most important position requirements *that you meet very well.* You will use them in the actual OBJECTIVE.

OBJECTIVE: PART THREE: <u>What Is YOUR Unique Contribution?</u>: Here is where you'll have your first opportunity to distinguish yourself from your competition.

💣 Companies frequently have needs they are not aware of, but as an alert employee or customer, I am certain you have recognized some.

💣 If you have identified such a need, it is one that is currently going unmet. This is great news! You now have the opportunity to make the company aware of their need AND present yourself as the solution to it.

To complete Part Three of the OBJECTIVE, *identify a critical need the company has in that job that you can satisfy.*

Here's an **example of a completed custom OBJECTIVE:**

OBJECTIVE: "Full-time permanent Admitting Office Department Secretary position with Seattle Viaduct Hospital, a business that values expert office computer skills, sound knowledge of standard business correspondence, and a gentle, welcoming personal style that puts nervous patients at ease."

After the recruiter reads that OBJECTIVE, particularly the last 12 words, can't you just see him or her pause to think for a moment, and then hear them say, *"Humm. That's right. It would be good if the person we hire could put nervous patients at ease. Yeah!"*

And just like that, your résumé moves out of the spaghetti pile and becomes the stand-alone meatball.

Broken down, **here are the three elements of the OBJECTIVE**:

PART ONE: The Position: *Full-time permanent Admitting Office Department Secretary position with Seattle Viaduct Hospital,*

PART TWO: **The Required Skills:** *a business that values expert office computer skills, sound knowledge of standard business correspondence,*

PART THREE: **Your Unique Contribution:** *and a gentle, welcoming personal style that puts nervous patients at ease.*

Let me give you three other examples of an OBJECTIVE that would immediately catch a recruiter's attention.

Examples Two and Three follow the same three-part formula.

Example 2:

OBJECTIVE: *"Full-time permanent lawn care position with Smith Property Management, Inc, a company that requires personal commitment, attention to detail, perfect attendance and immaculate grounds for tenants."*

Example 3:

OBJECTIVE: *"Third-shift warehousing position with Smith Shipping and Hauling, a company that needs a bondable, drug-free individual with 20 years of accident-free forklift driving, no Worker's Compensation injuries, and a can-do-let's-get-it-done attitude."*

While I'd prefer you didn't, I know there will be times when you will do a blanket mailing to companies or will send your résumé to a number of companies within an industry or to executive search firms. For those situations, this example may help.

Example 4:

OBJECTIVE: *"Full-time permanent Human Resources Director in a Philadelphia insurance company that wants their human resources department to measurably cut costs and improve profitability."*

So. Pretend you are the recruiter. Which OBJECTIVE would catch your attention and make you want to read more: Examples One through Four, or a generic OBJECTIVE that simply stated a position title, or was filled with air words focused on what the applicant wants?

I thought so, too.

Before we get into writing objectives, let me share an interesting hidden potential benefit you may get from using a clear and specific OBJECTIVE.

When I was a recruiter, I sorted résumés into three stacks: *Interested, Maybe,* and *Thanks-But-No-Thanks (TBNT)*

The ones that simply were not a good "fit," were vague, poorly written or were clearly shot-gunned ended up in the *TBNT* file. I kept the *Maybe* ones in reserve. And of course I jumped on the *Interested* ones like you would not believe.

Here's the point: In addition to the positions I was actively trying to fill, I generally always had one to two job requisitions that were hard to fill and for which my managers were not pressing me to fill immediately.

Many times, after I had screened a résumé into the *Interested* pile for the position an applicant had applied for, often during my initial reading of the résumé or during the phone screen interview, I learned other things that enabled me to interview and often hire them for one of the harder-to-fill requisitions.

They made more money and I closed out more requisitions. It happened all the time, and it all started with an effective OBJECTIVE. More about this later on.

Exercise: Writing Objectives

While the three elements of an effective OBJECTIVE are fresh in your mind, let's take a few minutes and practice what you have learned.

Following the three-part process, practice writing OBJECTIVES for several positions in which you are interested.

If you don't have anything specific in mind at the moment, make up a couple. Dedicate the most time to identifying **PART THREE** and wording it at tightly as possible.

When you've completed this exercise, please put it aside and we will proceed to **STEP 2.**

Step 2: Create and Draw from a Data Bank of your "Representative Professional Accomplishments" to customize your résumé each time you submit it.

💣 WHY?

The focus of a functional résumé is not on your job duties and responsibilities; it is on what YOU have ACCOMPLISHED.

This is not the time to be shy or modest. If you were part of a team, the recruiter will want to know that. BUT the recruiter is interested in YOU, not in the team. Be prepared to use **"I"** a lot in what you write and what you say.

The heart of a functional résumé is an **ACCOMPLISHMENTS DATA BANK** where you will hold your Representative Professional Accomplishments.

More about the Data Bank later in this section. For now, please just start thinking about keeping your accomplishments in a Data Bank.

First, however, I want to address a seriously damaging misconception many people have about themselves, and one that jeopardizes the effectiveness of a functional résumé.

"I haven't accomplished anything. I was just doing my job."

If you are one of those people, please stop right here, read the quote again and really think about what it means and what holding that belief says about you.

This section is the essence of the course, so I want to make sure you get it right.

If you are going to create an effective functional résumé and get all you can from what I can teach you, it is essential that you not only understand but really **believe** the next eleven words:

"DOING WHAT YOU ARE PAID TO DO MEANS YOU HAVE ACCOMPLISHMENTS."

Absolutely you are "doing your job," and ABSOLUTELY I will show you how to convert "Just Doing My Job" into ACCOMPLISHMENTS.

I want to convince you to never, ever again say "I was just doing my job" unless you're in a cowboy movie and you preface "I was just doing my job" with "Aw, shucks, ma'am…"

Let me emphasize this point with a story.

Some years back, I remember reading that Stephen Covey (author of *Seven Habits of Highly Effective People*) got into a taxi in New York, expecting it to be an unsanitary and uncomfortable experience.

He was astonished to find the interior spotless, the driver neatly and professionally attired in a suit and tie, offering an array of business services and niceties right there in his cab.

If a passenger needed to send a fax, or make a cell phone call, a professionally-lettered sign announced that he could do both. Thirsty? Another professionally lettered sign told passengers he had a cooler with cold drinks and a thermos of hot coffee, with cups, cream and sugar. Racks on the backs of both front seats held current magazines and neatly folded newspapers. To complete the service, two umbrellas were available and there were two reading lights for passengers to use, just like in a limo.

After an engaging conversation, Covey apologized for asking an indelicate question: Given how he ran his cab, what did the driver earn in comparison to his counterparts?

"I earn double," was the driver's answer.

Cab drivers drive people from point A to point B. Cab rides are a commodity service, and if you spoke with fifty drivers, my guess is that "just doing my job" would be how they would summarize what they do, with very little to differentiate one from the other.

And yet this man defined "just doing my job" very differently, and he was rewarded for it.
Viewed properly and with a little help, everyone can convert "just doing my job" into ACCOMPLISHMENTS that will make you money.

And in case you are wondering, this whole functional résumé process is not just for managers. I would absolutely love to write that cabbie's résumé!

A woman in one of my workshops had been a waitress in the same Interstate exit restaurant for 28 years and from one day to the next was laid off when the place closed. She applied what she learned in the workshop and within four weeks was invited for her first, and then second interviews, and then was hired at the region's prestigious new casino restaurant where she knows the tips will be much higher.

Another workshop participant, a woman who had retired after a thirty-year career in administration, thought she had retirement under control but the 2009 recession forced her back to work. She was dreading returning to her former field of employment; what she really wanted to do was tend the flowers in the garden shop of one of the big-box home improvement stores. She followed the format and I gave her some phone guidance. Five weeks later she wrote and told me she got the job.

Exercise:
Thinking about Your Accomplishments

I'd like you to ease into the whole accomplishments topic by thinking sitting back, closing your eyes and recalling things you have done that made you proud.

Please do not limit your thinking only to work-related accomplishments. The reason for this is that we will use your accomplishments to identify your most marketable skills, the ones you like to use and have used to achieve your most significant accomplishments. You may not be using them at work, but rather in your outside activities.

As an example of a significant accomplishment, one of my primary ones was successfully managing the shut-down and outplacement of a ninety-person office – on time, within budget, with no discrimination lawsuits and everyone found jobs equal to or better than the ones they lost.

For now, identify seven to ten of your most important ACCOMPLISHMENTS. The selection criteria are these:

You are most proud of them. They moved your reputation, your career, your department, your company or organization furthest down the road. These are the ones you would want placed on your tomb stone if you died tomorrow.

In other words: The Biggies.

Please grab that pad you have been keeping handy and jot down your primary accomplishments – no details right now – just identify your seven to ten most important accomplishments, and give each a title.

Converting "Activities" Into "Accomplishments"

All right. Maybe that went smoothly, or perhaps you had difficulty getting beyond your job duties and responsibilities and into thinking about the net result of what you have actually accomplished. Don't worry. What we are about to do should take care of it.

Let's turn our attention to converting activities and job duties into **ACCOMPLISHMENTS.**

💣 Let me give you some examples of regular job duties and activities that can easily be converted into ACCOMPLISHMENTS. These are not made up; I've had personal experience with people in each of these categories.

SECRETARY	CUSTOMER SERVICE
Reorganized files	Reduced average call time
Improved accuracy of phone message	Reduced escalations
Improved boss's productivity:	Transitioned customer service calls sales
Repetitive tasks	Number of customer compliments to my boss
Some meetings	Resolved customer objections without conflict
Gatekeeper	
Calendar management	
Budget analysis	
LAWN KEEPER	**MANAGER**
Suggest design ideas and materials owners had not considered	Supported company in community
Cost-conscious on owners' behalf	Maintained environment of personal motivation for staff
Suggest ways to reuse materials vs. haul away	Committed to making contributions
Completed project on time and under budget	Shared knowledge
	Actively mentored others

Brought in water specialist to solve drainage problem Gave homeowners before and after photos of final project Personal enthusiasm On time and brought good help	Saw needs going unmet / problems going unsolved: Took initiative Developed and implemented plan Championed plan with persistence Measurably achieved goals
HOME REPAIR Perfectionist If my work does not meet MY standards, will redo at no charge My work is my reputation Check back after work done: All working OK / to your satisfaction? Recommend most appropriate materials, not most expensive or cheapest Clean up daily Once fixed, it stays fixed	**INTERIOR HOUSE PAINTER** Offer color suggestions, rather than "whatever" Recommend best paint for job Meticulous care at wall and ceiling edges Critical eye for evenness Come back and do touch-ups after moving in. No Charge Genuinely happy person Follow-up call months later. Is everyone still happy?

"So What?"

I consider the bulk of those bullet points to be *activities (general)* that can be converted into *accomplishments (specific).*

Each bullet point is broad and rather general. For purposes of identifying our primary accomplishments, we need to **convert general** into **specific.**

You do that by first selecting an activity (any one of the bullet points) and then asking **"SO WHAT?"** several times. With each *"SO WHAT?"* your answers will become more and more specific.

Think of the process as a funnel – going from wide-open and general down to very specific. Or maybe descending a flight of steps until you get to the bottom.

When you find yourself repeating yourself or you have no more answers, you have arrived at your ACCOMPLISHMENT.

All that remains is to edit / polish it so it represents the essence of what you achieved.

Let's look at an example.

ACTIVITY:

"I do home repairs for people"	**"SO WHAT?"**
\ "Well, I work fast. I get in, get out and get to the next job."	**"SO WHAT?"**
\ "The faster I worked, the more focused I was. The more attention I paid, the more money I made. My number of NC (No Charge) calls to come back and redo my work dropped to zero. I have not had to do a redo in eleven months."	
That's how to go from ACTIVITY to ACCOMPLISHMENT.	☺

This is the **ACCOMPLISHMENT** that would go in your Accomplishments Data Bank and on the résumé:

"The faster I worked and more focused I was, the more attention I paid and the more money I made. My number of No Charge (NC) calls to come back and do touch-up

dropped to zero. I have not been called back for a redo in 11 months."

That's a long way from *"I do home repairs for people."*

Do you see how that worked? I have yet to find an activity that could not be converted into an accomplishment. There may be one out there, but I don't think so.

♠* Whether you are a CEO in Seattle or a taxi driver in New York or something someplace in between, please know that the *"SO WHAT?"* game will enable you to transform any ACTIVITY into an ACCOMPLISHMENT. Play on!

Power Words

One more thing before you get to begin writing your accomplishments. I'd like you to consider what are known as Power Words.

♠* I'm sure you *know*, but I want you to move beyond *knowing* and become <u>very aware</u>, that the words you use to describe your accomplishments tell discerning people a lot about how you see yourself.

When you think about your achievements, are the words you use *powerful and confident*, or are they *weak and passive*?

There are lots of ways to express a thought. Some words (like *Helped, Participated in* and *Assisted*) are not very active. In fact, they are passive and weak, and for our purposes, let's avoid them.

The ones in the following table are active, strong and vibrant and are appropriate for use in your ACCOMPLISHMENTS.

The list is not exhaustive, but it will certainly get you going. Feel free to add to the list with words of your own.

POWER WORDS LIST:

Accelerated	Developed	Launched	Resolved
Accomplished	Devised	Learned	Reviewed
Achieved	Drafted	Managed	Revised
Approved	Eliminated	Mentored	Saved
Assembled	Exemplified	Measurably	Streamlined
Authored	Facilitated	Monitored	Supervised
Authorized	Formulated	Negotiated	Taught
Coached	Gained	Operated	Tracked
Collaborated	Generated	Organized	Trained
Committed	Guaranteed	Overcame	**MY FAVORITE**
Constructed	Implemented	Presented	*Got 'er done!*
Completed	Improved	Produced	**WHAT OTHERS?**
Created	Increased	Raised	
Critiqued	Influenced	Reached	
Debugged	Initiated	Recovered	
Decreased	Innovated	Reduced	
Dedicated	Installed	Replaced	
Designed	Inventoried	Researched	

💣 A word of caution: It is certainly possible to overload a résumé with power words, to the point that it becomes comical. With attention and practice, you'll develop a sense of when the balance is right. Before you send out your first résumés, I recommend you get feedback from people whose experience and judgment you trust.

Exercise: Identifying Powerful Words that Describe You

💣 Please take a moment before going any further and make a copy of the POWER WORD LIST. In the narrow boxes to the left of the columns of words, put a little check by each of the words that accurately describe you in a work situation.

💣 Be certain to use in your résumé ONLY those words you can support because *anything you include in your résumé is fair game for the interviewer*. You definitely don't want to get caught in an overstatement or an unjustifiable accomplishment. (I hesitate to use the word "lie" and I know you get the point.)

Introduction to Exercise:
Writing your Accomplishments

All right!

You have:

- identified your seven to ten most significant accomplishments

- learned how to convert activities into accomplishments using *"SO WHAT?"*

- considered **POWER WORDS** and identified the ones that pertain to you.

Now it's time for you to get very focused and do some real thinking and writing.

It's time to WRITE ABOUT your accomplishments

💣💣💣 **This next point is absolutely critical.** _If you miss this point, you miss both the purpose and the power of all that we are doing._

I said "write about." I did NOT say "think about" seven to ten ACCOMPLISHMENTS essays.

This exercise is the guts of the course, and if you are going to get your money's worth, you must do it.

You don't need to be an expert writer to benefit from this exercise.

You don't need to have gotten A's in school when you had to write essays.

ALL you need to know how to do is just write.

Not necessarily write well. Just write.

If writing paragraphs makes your head explode, use bullet points.

If that does not work, find someone who will write or type your words as you say them.

Please. Do this.

Seven to ten accomplishments essays is the minimum, just to get started.

I would be thrilled if you would be an over-achiever, go 'way beyond the minimum and write 15 or 20 accomplishments essays so you would have a bunch on deposit in your **Accomplishments Data Bank.**

💣 WHY?

BECAUSE... *You are about to take the second step to making your functional résumé a unique document, tailored to present you as the most ideal candidate you can possibly be for each position for which you apply.*

That's pretty great!

You will definitely copy-and-paste some of the same accomplishments over and over, but *you will never again create and submit the same résumé for a variety of different positions*.

Using the SAME résumé for DIFFERENT positions is senseless and lazy and it helps keep you unemployed.

Rather, you will select and then copy-and-paste from your ACCOMPLISHMENTS or PROJECTS DATA BANK only those accomplishments that are most relevant to each position for which you are applying.

💣 This is important. I think in terms of ACCOMPLISHMENTS because that is how my career has evolved. If your career has been based on PROJECTS more than accomplishments, then by all means think "PROJECTS" when I speak of accomplishments and create your PROJECTS DATA BANK.

💣 **Have I mentioned that your success rests on** customizing the *OBJECTIVE, SPECIAL SKILLS AND ABILITIES,* and *REPRESENTATIVE PROFESSIONAL ACCOMPLISHMENTS* in your résumé *each time* you submit it?

Exercise:
Writing Your Accomplishments Essays

Now it is time for you to do some thinking and put your thoughts on paper.

All we are going to do now is write _essays_ for your seven to ten accomplishments.

We are NOT going to write the actual ACCOMPLISHMENTS that will end up in your résumés. We will take care of that in a bit.

As you get into this, you may find it helpful to think in terms of RESULTS AREAS. Here are some for your consideration. The list could be endless.

- Cost
- Time
- Rework
- Customer Comments
- Headcount Reduction
- Quality
- Market Share
- Profitability
- Productivity
- Personal

What others come to mind?

Please refer to your list of accomplishments. Please give each accomplishment a title and assign each a different color.

Now, find a quiet place where you will not be interrupted by family, phone or e-mail. Center yourself and compose your thoughts.

Give yourself and your career the benefit of some valuable solitude.

When you take the time to thoughtfully write each essay, you are preparing yourself for the job interview because you will have already thought about and answered at least 95% of what the interviewer will likely ask you.

Please write one 250-word essay per accomplishment. To put that into perspective, when you wrote a one-page essay in school, you wrote about 250 words.

Please answer these four questions *in each essay:*

1. *WHAT I did?*
2. *HOW I did it?*
3. *WHY I did it?*
4. *QUANTIFIED results of what I did?*

☛* **A WORD OF CAUTION:** Do not get so hung up on Question 4 that you skip the entire exercise. I don't know why, but some people do, to their detriment.

Once you have answered the first three questions, with some thought and maybe a little research into your old files or calling current or former colleagues, you can generally back into the numbers and answer Question Four.

And for both the résumé and the interview, it is perfectly fine to use the word "approximately." My only guideline is that you keep the quantified results reasonable, credible and easily explainable.

So please, don't cut corners anywhere in this course, and particularly here.

Take your time. Do the exercises and you'll reap the benefits.

And one more thing: as you are writing your essays, I'd like you to please make note of any special skills or abilities you used to achieve your accomplishments. Without losing your focus on your accomplishment essays, just jot them down in the margin or on the back of the page someplace, as they pop into your head. They'll be important when we identify your SPECIAL SKILLS AND ABILITIES.

Don't trust your memory. *Immediately* write them down. The ideas and thoughts will be fleeting and chances are you will not recall them later. Without going off on a tangent and getting lost in details, word them as specifically as possible.

I promise you'll thank me when you get to the section on SPECIAL SKILLS AND ABILITIES.

PLEASE TAKE AS MUCH TIME AS YOU NEED TO COMPLETE THIS EXERCISE.

PLEASE DO NOT PROCEED ANY FURTHER UNTIL YOU HAVE WRITTEN ALL OF YOUR ESSAYS.

Welcome Back!

Excellent! Excellent! If you have not patted yourself on the back for having completed all of your essays, please stand up and do so now!

And give yourself a round of applause while you're at it. YOU deserve it.

You DO deserve it, don't you?

If you have not completed all of your essays, you should not be reading this.

Please tweak the tip of your nose, then go back and complete your assignment.

I mean it.

GO!

ACORN
CONSULTING INC™

Welcome Back, *Again*

All right. Let's move on.

Exercise:
The Essence of Your Accomplishments

Please reread your first essay and then stop and think about *the essence* of what you have written.

Buried within those 250 words is **the essence of your accomplishment.** What is it?

Write a short three-to-five-sentence paragraph that describes the essence of what you did, including the quantifiable results.

You have now finished the **FIRST DRAFT** of an accomplishment.

This little paragraph, once you have edited it to make certain it accurately and succinctly describes your *achievement*, will ultimately become the accomplishment you will use in your functional résumé.

💣* As you finish writing each accomplishment, please play the *"SO WHAT?"* game. The purpose of the *SO WHAT?* game is to make sure you are not describing an ACTIVITY but rather have gotten to the essence of the ACCOMPLISHMENT.

SPECIAL INSTRUCTION: After applying *"SO WHAT?"* make whatever edits or corrections you feel are necessary, then place that accomplishment into your ACCOMPLISHMENTS DATA BANK. Don't worry about its organization right now. We'll get to that next.

Now please move on and finish writing the rest of your accomplishments.

….. Time passes while you think and write, until at last I can say to you…

Congratulations! You still have a ways to go before you are done, but you have definitely completed the major challenge of the book! The rest is a piece of cake.

Your Accomplishments Data Bank

REMEMBER: Everything we are doing is intended to make your résumé stand out from the competition. That is easy to do when you hold your accomplishments in your ACCOMPLISHMENTS DATA BANK and *copy-and-paste only those that are relevant to the position for which you are applying.*

✒* And I reiterate, for this strategy to work, you will need to modify your OBJECTIVE, your REPRESENTATIVE PROFESSIONAL ACCOMPLISHMENTS and your SPECIAL SKILLS AND ABILITIES each time, based on *the unique requirements for each position for which you are applying.*

By now you may be groaning either *"All right already. I get it"* or maybe you are saying, *"NO WAY! Too much work!"*

If you're feeling some resistance, please take a deep breath and keep the faith. Once you understand the process, using your ACCOMPLISHMENTS DATA BANK is easy.

💣 For the ACCOMPLISHMENTS DATA BANK to work effectively, you will need to commit to keeping it current, adding new accomplishments as you achieve them. When you need the accomplishment, it is much easier to refer to something you have written down when it was fresh, rather than try to remember and recreate from memory.

💣 I know I've shown you how to convert an activity into an accomplishment. Now, let me tell you a brief story intended to show you how to recognize an accomplishment.

Someone I've known for years was hired shortly before the 2008 recession. When her company announced that upcoming department layoffs would be based on *last-in / first-out* and they would be offering packages to those who volunteered, she raised her hand because she was last-in and just wanted to get on with it.

Imagine her surprise when the company rejected her, saying that even though she was last-in, she was too valuable for lay-off. They wanted to keep her and had a job for her when the company completed its reorganization.

Without question, that's an accomplishment and it belongs in her ACCOMPLISHMENTS DATA BANK, ready for copy-and-paste use when appropriate.

Can you imagine the powerful impact that accomplishment will have on a recruiter when they read her resume?

"Wow! Her company made special accommodations just to keep her. Get her in here – NOW!!"

That's how it is when your accomplishments resonate with a recruiter: you jump to the top of the pile as the competition melts away. Your accomplishments are everywhere. Be alert and pay attention to find them.

Organizing Your Accomplishments: Subcategories and Key Words

Another of the primary differences between a functional résumé and many reverse-chronological ones is the use of **Subcategories.**

Subcategories are a key element in the REPRESENTATIVE PROFESSIONAL ACCOMPLISHMENTS section in a functional résumé, and generally not used in reverse-chronological résumés.

💣※ Given that many résumés are screened in or out of contention by computer programs that search for "Key Words" related to the position, you will want to precisely tailor your résumé to the position for which you are applying. You do that by including "key words" taken from the *requirements listed in the position description or elsewhere within the position announcement.*

You include the key words in both your subcategories as well as your accomplishments

Of course, if the position for which you are applying has no written qualifications, select your ACCOMPLISHMENTS and SUBCATEGORIES based on what you know from experience about the requirements of the job.

In no particular order, here are some of the more frequently-used subcategories I have seen used effectively.

- Cost Control
- Process Improvement
- Time Management
- Customer Relations
- Attention to Detail
- Manual Dexterity
- Planning
- Personal Flexibility
- Personal Initiative
- Personal Commitment
- Community Relations
- Mentoring
- Management Development
- Market Growth

The list of possible **SUBCATEGORIES** is just about endless. The ones you select will be determined by the position for which you are applying.

Recapping Accomplishments

This is by far the most difficult element of the course.

Here are the main points we have covered:

- Thinking about your accomplishments
- Converting activities into accomplishments by playing the "So What?" game
- Power Words
- Identifying powerful words that describe you
- Writing your accomplishments essays
- Accomplishments data banks
- Using subcategories and key words to organize your accomplishments

STEP 3: Create and draw from a Data Bank of your "Special Skills and Abilities" to customize your résumé each time you submit it.

WHY?

By now, you already know the answer. Because you don't want to waste a **SPECIFIC opportunity** by casually tossing a **GENERIC résumé** at it. You want to tailor your skills and abilities to the requirements of *each job* for which you are applying.

Special Skills and Abilities

All too often we impose our own very artificial and unwarranted limits on the positions we think we can do.

We think that since we have always done one particular job, that's all we're qualified to do.

Wrong. Absolutely wrong.

As we determine your SPECIAL SKILLS AND ABILITIES, you will identify **your "transferrable skills."**

As the name suggests, these are skills that are transferrable from one position or industry to another position or industry.

💣※ **Please don't go all "yeah, sure" on me and close down. What we are about to cover may be the most important "Ah-HA!" of the entire course.**

"What are some of your SPECIAL SKILLS AND ABILITIES?"

♣* If the interviewer asked you that, (and it would be a very fair question,) how would you answer it?

♣* If your immediate response would be to tell them about your high school or college courses, what you did in the military, or about your current job duties and responsibilities, where you were born or your formative years, you would be shooting yourself in the foot and missing a tremendous opportunity to instantaneously distance yourself from the competition.

♣* If you have done your homework by relating your qualifications to those of the position for which you are applying, you have prepared yourself to knock the question, *"What are some of your special skills or abilities?"* right out of the park.

♣* *Your education, military experience and job duties, all of that, while important, is not what the recruiter is looking for. All of those are the* <u>activities</u> *in which you have been involved over the years. They are what you have* <u>done</u>; *they are not your SPECIAL SKILLS AND ABILITIES.*

Consider it from this perspective:

You Are Much More Than the Sum of Your Work History and Job Skills.

William Bridges, change management expert and author of several books including my personal favorite, **Creating You & Co**. (an extremely valuable book for you as you go about your search for work), affirms that "jobs" as the best way to get work done are going away. For proof, he cites down-sizing, outsourcing, right-sizing and working virtually.

According to Bridges, the trick is to learn not just to survive but to THRIVE in what he calls today's "dejobbed" world.

When I accept a client for outplacement and résumé assistance, I ask them to get a copy of *Creating You & Co.*, read it and actually do the exercises. I want them to become aware of the SPECIAL SKILLS AND ABILITIES that they really bring to what Bridges termed "the World of Work."

One client had been self-employed for forty years, and suddenly hit a wall. He stopped getting contracts. His résumé was a disaster, and before we got to work on it, I had him read and do the exercises in **Creating You & Co.**

He dedicated a long weekend to the task, and when he finished, he told me he had learned more about himself in that three-day period than he had in the past forty years. He thought that was a plus for the book and a pretty sad commentary on his life.

The book is out of print, but is available on-line. I urge you to get it and read it. You will not regret it.

And in case you are wondering, we got his career back on track.

More About What You Bring to the "World of Work"

♦※ As I recall, Bridges earned his Ph.D. in Literature from Yale, and then began to teach literature. After a few short years, he found himself in an unhappy repetitive loop.

Taking stock of himself, he asked himself what he could do? Teach literature. Who made up his circle of friends? Other professors.

Trapped but really smart, he began researching and put together a workshop to help people who were stuck get from where they were in life (Point A) to where they wanted to be (Point B).

He focused on helping people *thrive*, not just survive, in the gap between points A and B. In the process, he built himself a decades-long noteworthy international consulting career as an expert in change management, helping individuals and companies manage their transitions across the gap from Point A to Point B.

Creating You & Co. is his blueprint for thriving in today's "dejobbed" world.

One of the primary exercises in that book is determining what special skills and abilities you bring to the "world of work."

Using himself as a guinea pig, he analyzed himself as far back as high school. Summarizing, he realized he possessed these *special skills and abilities*:

- He learned quickly
- He could apply what he learned in new and different circumstances
- He had effective influencing and communication skills, both written and oral
- He could persuade others to his way of thinking
- He got on well with all the guys - the ones on the chess team as well as the jocks, and all the guys in between
- He got on well with the girls too, and they did not scare him.

💣 **Here's the point.** Bridges said that none of those items appear on his résumé, *BUT THEY ARE RESPONSIBLE FOR ALMOST EVERYTHING THAT DOES.*

💣* Did you get the importance of that last sentence? If you skipped over it, please reread it and think seriously about its relevance to you as you seek work.

Those were some of his SPECIAL SKILLS AND ABILITIES.

They set him apart. They are what he realized he brought to "the World of Work."

What do YOU bring to the "World of Work?"

That is a difficult question to thoroughly answer.

After you have completed your ACCOMPLISHMENTS essays and finalized your actual accomplishments, you'll have only one more significant challenge: to complete two different **SKILLS EXERCISES,** and then you'll be able to answer that question, with great clarity.

For now, let me take you back to my earlier ACCOMPLISHMENT example.

Remember this one?

"The faster I worked and more focused I was, the more attention I paid and the more money I made. My number of No Charge (NC) calls to come back and do touch-up dropped to zero. I have not been called back for a redo in 11 months."

If that was *your* accomplishment, what *skills* would you say you used?

Here are some I think you might have used:

- Attention to detail   *what* you were doing
- Manual dexterity   *how you were* doing it

67

- Planning   _when_/sequence of steps followed
- Time management   _how_ you spent your time
- Flexible approach   _what_ was and was not working; paid attention; made adjustments

How to Identify Your Special Skills and Abilities

💣 In order to thoroughly identify your **SPECIAL SKILLS AND ABILITIES**, you'll first need to have written your ACCOMPLISHMENTS essays.

However, if while you were writing your accomplishments essays you honored my request that you make note of the skills you used, you'll already have a head-start on identifying your SPECIAL SKILLS AND ABILITIES.

Those little thoughts were flashes of inspiration and your notes will now be helpful as you identify which skills and abilities you used as you achieved each accomplishment.
For example, let's say _"Good with people"_ popped into your head while you are writing an accomplishment essay.
"Good with people" sounds like you would want to use it, doesn't it? But when you stop and think about it, you'll realize it is very vague, and therefore of little value for us.

Immediately after writing down _"good with people,"_ you might have asked yourself what that really meant and how you could make it more specific? Maybe _"Put new-hires rapidly at ease"_ came to mind. This is more specific, and the more specific things are, the more useful they are.

Could you make _"Put new-hires rapidly at ease"_ even more specific?

Play the "SO WHAT?" game until you can go no further. If nothing else comes to you, go with it because it is more useful than "good with people."

PLEASE NOTE: As I typed *"put new-hires rapidly at ease,"* the thought popped into my mind that in addition to being a skill, it could also be a topic for an accomplishments essay.
If that had been your idea, to determine if it is worth an essay, you would apply the "SO WHAT?" test and see where it leads you.

If what you came up with made sense, you would write another essay. If what you came up with is not that important, keep it for SPECIAL SKILLS AND ABILITIES.

Either way, you win.

The point is to be alert and capture the quick flashing thoughts that will come to you. Keep that pad handy.

There are many resources on the Internet to help you identify your "transferrable skills," your SPECIAL SKILLS AND ABILITIES, as well as what are known as your **"Motivated Skills."**

The first is this link:
http://www.stewartcoopercoon.com/jobsearch/freejobsearcht ests.phtml.

I found it on http://www.jobhuntersbible.com/, the website of Richard Bolles, author of **What Color Is Your Parachute?,** the most comprehensive job search book I know. You will find it worthwhile to purchase the book, visit both links, and complete the exercise.

The second resource is more extensive. It is an exercise adapted from an earlier edition of Bolles' *What Color Is Your Parachute?*

Preliminary Instructions: *If you have not finished writing your accomplishments essays and then writing your actual accomplishment, please stop now and do so now. You must have finished both halves of that exercise in order to effectively complete this next one.*

Exercise: Identifying Your Transferrable Skills (Adapted from *What Color Is Your Parachute?* by Richard Bolles/2001 ed. www.JobHuntersBible.com)

Give each of your accomplishments essays a title and assign it a different color. Then, working only on one essay at a time, read each skill in turn, and if you used it in the achievement of your accomplishment, put a ✔ in the corresponding color in the appropriate box. After you have completed the first essay, follow the same process for your remaining essays.

When you have finished all of your essays, you will see a profile of the transferrable skills and abilities you have used to achieve your most significant accomplishments.

Don't be surprised if twenty or thirty have a lot of checks. NEXT, please review all the skills that have the most ✔ s and identify nine to twelve that you most enjoy using. These are your *MOTIVATED SKILLS*... you get the most satisfaction when you use then AND you achieve your most significant results when you use them.

You will present your motivated skills in your résumé. When you begin your job search, you will be looking for jobs or work that requires the use of your motivated skills.

In addition to this exercise, you can identify more skills by at this site, (a link from Richard Bolles' site): http://www.stewartcoopercoon.com/jobsearch/freejobsearchtests.phtml.

Give yourself time, and have fun learning about yourself!

Please give each of your accomplishment essays a title and assign a different color for each essay.

1_____
2_____
3_____
4_____
5_____
6_____
7_____
8_____
9_____

	1	2	3	4	5	6	7	8	9
USING YOUR BODY:									
Manual dexterity									
Precise eye-hand coordination									
Physical stamina & agility									
High tolerance for discomfort/pain in warm or cold environment									
Excellent hearing, vision, sense of smell, touch, taste									
WORKING WITH:									
TOOLS									
Hammering, sawing									
Sewing, knitting									
Cutting									

	1	2	3	4	5	6	7	8	9
Sculpting									
Painting, finishing									
OBJECTS									
Washing, cleaning									
Expedite / fill orders									
Preparing food									
Repair, restoration									
Lifting, pulling, hauling, carrying									
HEAVY EQUIPMENT									
Readying, putting together									
Driving (manual / remote control)									
Maintenance									
Taking apart / putting together									
CONSTRUCTION									
Building									
Remodeling									
CARING FOR									
Plants									
Animals									
Children / Seniors									
USING YOUR MIND:									
RESEARCHING DATA									
Researching									
Interviewing, observing									
Exceptional math or verbal skills									
Exceptional memory									
Conceptualizing new ideas, creating or designing									

	1	2	3	4	5	6	7	8	9
MANAGING									
Analyzing, comparing									
Using computers									
Developing computer hardware									
Developing computer software									
Accounting									
Higher math									
Planning, laying out step-by-step process									
Creative thoughts, solutions									
Practical thoughts, solutions									
Organizing, data storage									
Developing strategies									
Executing strategies									
Providing counsel on strategies									
Influencing decision-makers									
Give-and-Take, Negotiating									
Authorizing actions, taking final responsibility									
Following through, tracking results									
Creating media presentations									
Conflict resolution									
Synthesizing, summarize data									
Design, conduct, evaluate training results									

	1	2	3	4	5	6	7	8	9
DATA MANAGEMENT									
Cataloguing, record keeping									
Information clearing-house, data retrieval									
INTERPERSONAL SKILLS:									
WITH INDIVIDUALS									
Carrying out orders, repetitive procedures									
Communicating effectively in person									
Communicate effectively in writing									
Communicate effectively electronically									
Tutoring, mentoring, coaching									
Diagnosing performance problems									
Networking, connecting people with others, resources									
Recruiting, assessment, selection									
Selling services, products for money									
Foreign language skill – speak, read, write, understand, translate, interpret									
WITH LARGE/SMALL GROUPS									
Clarity of expression									
Effective presentations									
Holds listeners' attention									

	1	2	3	4	5	6	7	8	9
Entertaining manner									
Performing									
Leading exercises and games									
Technical consulting									
Project management / coordination									
Convincing a group to accept your ideas									
Effective facilitator of group to draw out ideas									

All right. You have now identified your "Transferrable Skills."
They will "transfer" from one job or career to another

With an open mind and creative thought, you will be able to
identify other companies / industries where those skills will
be relevant and valued.

Please note your transferrable skills, perhaps as a subset of
your SPECIAL SKILLS AND ABILITIES DATA BANK.

Exercise:
Identifying Your MOTIVATED SKILLS

Your MOTIVATED SKILLS are the skills you love to use,
and when you use them, you get your best results.

Please go back through your transferrable skills and identify
your nine to twelve more important MOTIVATED SKILLS.

Record them in the chart below.

MY MOTIVATED SKILLS, THE ONES I REALLY LOVE TO USE, ARE:

Special Skills and Abilities Data Bank

After you have written your accomplishments essays and completed the above exercise, as you look across all four pages of different colored check marks, I am certain you will see that you possess a significant number of skills and abilities, perhaps some of which you were unaware.

Once you have identified them all, please transfer them into a separate WORD or EXCEL document – your **SPECIAL SKILLS AND ABILITIES DATA BANK,** *and make the commitment to yourself to keep this data bank current.*

💣 Please remember that, as with your ACCOMPLISHMENTS, you will never use all of your SPECIAL SKILLS AND ABILITIES at once in any one résumé. Based on the requirements of each position you are seeking, you will copy-and-paste into your résumé only the most relevant special skills and abilities for each job**.**

Don't be surprised if you have identified at least twenty special skills and abilities that you have used repeatedly. Include them all into this **DATA BANK.**

Out of all the skills and abilities you have identified, there will be only a handful, maybe ten or twelve, core skills that you love to use, that give you great satisfaction to use, and that you use repeatedly to achieve your most significant results. Identify them in the small table at the end of the exercise, above.

Those are called your **MOTIVATED SKILLS**. Please create a **MOTIVATED SKILLS DATA BANK** and keep your very special skills and abilities in there. Update this data bank as needed.

Your **MOTIVATED SKILLS** are the essence of what you bring to the "World of Work" and if you have identified them beforehand, you will find many opportunities during your job search to present them in your cover letters and during interviews.

Speaking from personal experience, it was always more impressive when a job candidate could smoothly tell me about their most significant skills, and give me examples to support their claims, rather than say, "uh, gee," and then look at the wall for an answer.

Recapping Special Skills and Abilities

♦*♦*♦* Each time you submit your functional résumé for a new position, in order to present yourself as the ideal candidate, you will customize your:

- OBJECTIVE
- REPRESENTATIVE PROFESSIONAL ACCOMPLISHMENTS
- SPECIAL SKILLS AND ABILITIES

in accordance with the requirements of each new position.

Other Categories of Your Résumé

But what about the rest of the résumé – the boilerplate elements that remain constant from one résumé to the next – work history, education, outside interests - and like that?

After having presented your OBJECTIVE, SPECIAL SKILLS AND ABILITIES, and REPRESENTATIVE PROFESSIONAL

ACCOMPLISHMENTS, present your next-most-relevant category.

Most often, that will be either your **WORK EXPERIENCE** or **EDUCATION**.

Here's the thing: After customizing your OBJECTIVE, SPECIAL SKILLS AND ABILITIES and ACCOMPLISHMENTS, from here on in, the sequence in which you present your information is up to you because by now either you have hooked the recruiter's interest, or you haven't. If you've followed my recommendations, my bet is that you will have.

In addition to WORK EXPERIENCE and EDUCATION, here are some other categories you may wish to include:

- CONTINUING EDUCATION
- SPECIAL TRAINING AND CERTIFICATIONS
- LICENSES
- MILITARY
- INTERNSHIPS

I like to include **OUTSIDE INTERESTS** as the final category in the functional résumés that I create.

Why? Because I learned a long time ago that an effective résumé will present as many interesting and relevant facets of the person as possible, until the person can speak personally on their own behalf.

A quick story. When I finished graduate school and began looking for a job, my father put my résumé together for me. He told me to include **OUTSIDE INTERESTS** as the final component. I asked him why I would want to do that, because I thought outside interests were personal and therefore not part of the résumé.

Dad told me that what people included there was the last thing the reader read and the applicant could sometimes establish a kind of personal link with the recruiter. He called it "remote control." That made sense to me and since I was seriously into photography, I included it.

A family friend thought I'd fit in Marriott Hotels and opened a door for me. They liked what they saw in my résumé because they called me for an interview. It lasted twelve hours, and when I left, I walked out with a job offer to become a human resources director (actually, back then it was called a personnel director) in one of their hotels.

As we were wrapping up, I noticed the interviewer had circled "photography" about 41 times in red ink and I asked him why. He told me he was into photography and it caught his eye. *Hmmmm.* He also told me that, while not a job requirement, given all the employee activities in the hotel, it was a plus for the property HR director to know how to use a camera.

Positive connection. Remote control. Convinced? Hope so.

Dad knew what he was about.

Feel free to organize the boilerplate sections of your résumé as you see fit.

With your **ACCOMPLISHMENTS** and **SKILLS Data Banks** complete, and knowing how to customize your **OBJECTIVE,** you are just about set to step out and make yourself the ideal candidate, the solution to needs going unmet.

CONGRATULATIONS! You now understand the nuts-and-bolts of how to write a functional résumé.

Next up – **Sample Functional Résumés.**

Sample Functional Résumés

William Bridges attributed the following quote to a former executive of DEC and he included it in **Creating You & Co.:**

> *"Just because a company does not have a job for you does not mean they don't have work for you."*

As you study the following functional résumé styles, please keep this quote in mind and think about becoming the solution to unmet needs.

By the end of this section, I will have shown you my three different formats for a functional résumé. The three formats are:

- *Narrative*
- *One-Page + Addendum*
- *Technical + Narrative*

Narrative Format:

Introduction to Selectivity Exercise: Using Your Data Banks

For purposes of this exercise, "Selectivity" refers to which accomplishments and which special skills and abilities to leave in the Data Banks for future use, and which to select and copy-and-paste into a new résumé.

You'll be practicing with the basic format - the *NARRATIVE*.

With her permission, you'll be working with the actual ACCOMPLISHMENTS and SPECIAL SKILLS AND

ABILITIES DATA BANKS that a colleague and I developed for her own job search.

When you have completed the exercise, I'll share her actual résumé with you and you'll be able to see how your selections compared with what she used for her search.

♦* To remind you once more: with so many people in the job market, in order for YOUR phone to ring with someone calling YOU for an interview, your résumé must stand out.

You might be interested in knowing that even with all the layoffs during the recession of 2008 - 2009, even though she has accepted a new position within her company and is not presently on the market, her functional résumé is still generating calls from referrals, recruiters, and those who knew she was looking.

♦* Remember, in order to package yourself as the best candidate for each position you will apply for, you will never submit a one-size-fits-all generic résumé for multiple positions.

Rather, based on the requirements for each position, you will select from your Data Banks your most relevant ACCOMPLISHMENTS and SPECIAL SKILLS AND ABILITIES for each position for which you apply.

So, regarding ACCOMPLISHMENTS and SPECIAL SKILLS AND ABILITIES DATA BANKS, the question becomes *"what to leave in and what to leave out?"*

Here is her actual Objective.

OBJECTIVE: *A full-time, permanent Marketing management position where I will be expected to analyze marketing problems, identify needs, develop and implement creative* *and profitable solutions, be held accountable for the results, and rewarded accordingly*

Right off the bat, you'll notice that her OBJECTIVE is not company-specific. This is because she used the résumé with a broadcast letter to seek *referrals* among people in her personal network. (More about referrals and cover letters in the Bonus Section.)

Exercise:
Selectivity / Using Your Data Banks

As you get into the exercise, imagine you are a recruiter and you have just read her *Objective*. Think for a moment about what *Special Skills and Abilities* and what *Representative Professional Accomplishments* you might expect to see in her résumé.

Remember, as you read through her Data Banks, some of her *Accomplishments* and *Special Skills* will be more relevant to her *Objective* than others.

💣 The purpose of this exercise is to analyze the contents of both Data Banks, then select and include only those *Special Skills* and *Accomplishments* that relate most directly to the needs and responsibilities of a marketing management position.

Before starting, I suggest you create a template like the one on page 99.

Her **SKILLS DATA BANK** contains twenty skills. Please select between nine and twelve that you feel would compliment her *Objective*. Note the ones you would copy-and-paste into each of the boxes of the table. Give thought to how you would organize them for maximum impact.

Her *ACCOMPLISHMENTS Data Bank* contains twenty-three accomplishments.

💣 In order to effectively present your *ACCOMPLISHMENTS*, you will need to organize them into subcategories. If you were applying for a specific position, your subcategories would be the primary areas of responsibility listed in the position description and you would slot the accomplishments you selected into those categories.
💣 However, since in this exercise you are not applying for a specific position but rather are *seeking referrals* from a number of people, you'll have to create your own *subcategories* and decide which REPRESENTATIVE PROFESSIONAL ACCOMPLISHMENTS will most effectively support your Marketing *OBJECTIVE.*

The best way to accomplish that is to do this:

As you read through her accomplishments, jot down two or three words that describe the essence of the accomplishment. Two possible ones could be *"Profitability through Planning"* and *"Marketing Creativity."* I'm sure you will think of many others.

💣 After you have read all of her accomplishments and made your topic notations, group them into similar categories. Then give each separate category a descriptive name, one that you believe would be picked up if someone put the résumé through a Key Word Search.

💣 Remember, your résumé could be in a stack of résumés that is seventeen inches high. To be read, it has to **stand out.**

💣 *Please remember: you only have the first ¾ of the first page (maybe seven to ten seconds) to capture the reader's interest so that they want to read on.*

💣 That means you want to have communicated your *OBJECTIVE* and *SPECIAL SKILLS AND ABILITIES* and begin telling the reader about your *ACCOMPLISHMENTS* by half-way down the first page.

💣 To grab and hold their interest, you must be certain to open the *Accomplishments* section with your most impressive, powerful and relevant accomplishments that compliment your OBJECTIVE.

*The **OBJECTIVE** once more:* *A full-time, permanent Marketing management position where I will be expected to analyze marketing problems, identify needs, develop and implement creative and profitable solutions, be held accountable for the results, and rewarded accordingly*

All right! Let's go identify some **SPECIAL SKILLS AND ABILITIES** and some **REPRESENTATIVE PROFESSIONAL ACCOMPLISHMENTS.**

Data Bank: Special Skills and Abilities

1. Marketing creativity

2. Event creativity

3. Written creativity

4. Committed to achieving and maintaining consistently high levels of client satisfaction

5. Hold high expectations for my own performance; strive for high levels of personal achievement

6. Maintain poise and self-confident composure in free-flowing situations; adjust and thrive in new environments

7. Quick study; able to apply what I have learned and work effectively without supervision

8. Routinely achieve profit objectives while working within established budgets

9. Confident when faced with learning new software and computer applications

10. Consensus builder; strong personal influencing skills; rapidly put people at ease and build trust

11. Enjoy interaction with people of diverse cultures, social and economic backgrounds

12. Take initiative to create pragmatic, effective solutions to business problems

13. Have been told repeatedly that I am mature and competent beyond my age

14. Committed to continuous learning and personal growth

15. Happy person, committed to both my colleagues and my company

16. Effective at balancing multiple projects and seeing them through to completion

17. Unafraid to speak my mind, directly and politely

18. Willing to make a decision and see it through

19. Take personal responsibility for my actions

20. Build and maintain lasting friendships

Data Bank: Representative Professional Accomplishments

💣 ***Reminder:*** *There are no subcategories in this Accomplishments Data Base. Using the unique qualifications of each position for which you are applying, you will create relevant subcategories for each position's résumé, then select the most relevant accomplishments and copy-and-paste them into the appropriate subcategories.*

1. During my first New Home Open House program, I wondered: *"Why do we devote two whole pages to an ineffective map when each home listing is equipped with directions?"* No one could answer that question for me since they'd been doing it that way for a while, so I created an alternative, which the newspaper adopted and still uses to this day. My solution was to group homes located in the same region together to make it easier for the reader to find homes in areas they are interested in; it encouraged the listing agent to offer a web address for more information and it returned the back two pages of the map to the advertising sales staff as additional space they could sell for revenue generation. (Newspaper)

2. As Member Relations Director, I managed a number of member committees. The *"Women on the Move"* committee was one of my most committed and dynamic. Within the company, I know of at least five sister Clubs that have copied my design. It has been a very successful forum for building political and community relations. The relationship of which I am most proud is the one we have established with Borders Books. On my initiative, I contacted their regional marketing director and we have formed an ongoing relationship bringing visiting authors to speak at dinner events at the Club. It has been a popular win/win for Borders, the authors, my members, and the Club. (Business Club)

3. Clay Aiken's Foundation approached the Club to partner with them in a fundraiser for charity. We accepted their offer, and I was responsible for marketing the event. Within one month, we had sold out the event to the maximum capacity of our facility. Working with his Foundation, I developed marketing pieces, helped design and write ad copy for our newsletter and members' website (both of which I wrote and maintained), developed and implemented an e-mail and poster campaign for the Club, and facilitated an introduction to the local newspaper's Features Editor. This was the first event of this kind we have done and it was a stellar success; over 50 members participated and we raised over $300,000 for his foundation, which enables summer camps for kids with special needs. (Business Club)

4. New to my job, I analyzed my accounts and requested a current run of spending reports. I noticed that several accounts had been spending well over their contracted amount as they advertised with the newspaper. I approached these accounts about signing a new contract at a level equal with their spending. Every one of the six accounts I approached with this option thanked me for my diligence and signed their new and higher contract levels. This resulted in an additional $40K in revenues for my newspaper win-win for the newspaper as well as the client.

By signing a higher contract level, the newspaper could count on the client achieving this higher level of spending for the next year and the client could count on the newspaper to supply them with lower rates than they had been receiving before. They could advertise more often and still spend the same. One of these accounts had previously been my manager's when she had been a sales person. I encouraged this account to sign at a level which was double what they had done before. They did and both my manager and her manager congratulated me for doing what my manager had been unable to do. (Newspaper)

5. Harry Potter. Timed with the release of one of the movies, we put on a themed adult/child dinner that included tickets to the movie at the IMAX across the street. We decorated and organized the dining room to look like the Hogwarts dining hall with four long tables based on the four houses in the Harry Potter books. When members came with a child, the child was placed under the Sorting Hat and I had someone with a great voice backstage calling out the names of the Houses, according to where we had seated them for their reservation. The dinner, the room decorations, everything worked to perfection and the members and their children loved it. One member loved it so much that he asked to speak personally with the person who created it – me! When we meet now, he calls me "Harry Potter." He asked me how long I will remain with the Club because Disney needs to pick me up sometime soon! (Business Club)

6. Members consistently praise the Club for the innovative activities I developed: the Harry Potter themed dinner, other themed dinners relating to IMAX movies, a private after-hours tour of the Titanic exhibit at the Museum of History ending in a black tie dinner at the Club featuring the menu of the final dinner served aboard the Titanic (members still talk about it three years later). Limousine scavenger hunts through Raleigh, stopping in several different restaurants to get clues for the hunt. Trips to the Art Museum for our Art Committee complete with lunch and a docent-led private tour. The list is extensive and member satisfaction ratings significant. It is gratifying to know how well received my work has been and the

positive image it has created for us in the community. (Business Club)

7. I like to design/create marketing solutions that are cost-effective, simple, and aesthetically pleasing. For the last five years, I have been responsible for all aspects of the publication of the Club's bi-monthly newsletter. I taught myself Quark and performed all layout, design, writing and photography. After several issues, I realized that the process was taking too much of my time, and I decided to see if the Corporate graphics designers could do the work, thereby expediting the process while saving me time and money. They were delighted to help, and by using their services and more advanced software, my design time went from two weeks to two days, and the cost (excluding postage) went from $1,800 per month to $756 – an annual savings of $12,528 for the Club and approximately 300 hours a year for the Club and for me. (Business Club)

8. As a result of a corporate acquisition and reorganization in January 2007, some of my original Director of Member Relations job duties shifted and I assumed half the responsibilities of a laid-off Private Events director. My new title was Food and Beverage Director of Sales, and I had a $1.5 million sales plan to meet, one that was based on aggressive increases in both food and beverage prices as well as revenue targets. Since there was no marketing plan for this position, the first thing I did upon acquiring this new responsibility was to create and implement a comprehensive one, because up to this point, Private Events had simply relied on word-of-mouth. Four months into the year, we are on track to make plan. (Business Club)

9. For all of 2006, I was personally responsible for the Club's retention of members. January began with a 72% retention level, and by year-end, we had improved it to 78%. That 6% increase was a hard-fought victory in a small and already-saturated market and it placed us in the top 20% of all of the Clubs. I was recognized for this achievement. To achieve this accomplishment, I developed and implemented a variety of creative and well-received activities and events that were successful in (1) getting honest feedback about why members were not renewing, and (2) educating and convincing a significant portion of members to maintain / renew their memberships. (Business Club)

10. Founding member of Club's Chapter Toastmasters International. In response to Member interest, researched the organization and managed all aspects of the creation and certification of the chapter. As of May 2007, the Chapter had 22 Members. The Chapter had attained the highest performance designation of President's Distinguished Club. Served in elected role as VP of Education May 2002 to June 2003 (Business Club)

11. With only three months experience and only minimal training in my new job, my colleague / peer who was supposed to train me left the club, leaving me as the sole Private Event Director. I met the challenge head-on with a positive attitude tackling it through 13 hour days and six day a week work schedule. One colleague commented that she wasn't sure how I managed to do it with a smile on my face every day. I surpassed budget for each month. Period 5 was the largest; The Private Event plan was $118,000; I exceed it by $29,000 with a final total of $149,000. I executed each event perfectly, without dropping a single ball. (Business Club)

12. The Member Relations Director position planned and sold events based on what the members were interested in. However, at times I created and hosted events that were off everyone's radar screens, i.e. Chocolate Brunches, dance classes paired with a big dance event, Chocolate and Wine tastings, Scotch tastings and Hurricane Voo-Doo parties to ward off bad hurricanes. Because I was never afraid of trying something new, I constantly sold not just events, but new ideas and change to Club members, my own staff and Club management. I'm proud to say I always received the support I needed to make each new idea a success. (Business Club)

13. Due to resignations, terminations, and transfers of managers and supervisors, as well as higher-than-normal turnover among staff, our Club was in a constant state of change and turmoil for over two years. While somewhat uncomfortable, I am flattered that because of the relationships I had made with many of my members, a number of them have come to me to personally to share their concerns, rather than gossiping and complaining among themselves. Their trust gave me a number of opportunities to conduct damage control, and I know of at least six members that I was able to retain as a result of having established strong personal as well as professional relationships. (Business Club)

14. Over the last five years, I have become good friends with many of our members, and when one of them, a man in his 60s, suddenly found himself in the job market, he asked a number of people for a letter attesting to his character, including me. I was honored and touched that this man, more than twice my age, thought enough of me to ask for a letter. He later reported to me with deep gratitude that the letter I wrote was instrumental in

helping him secure a new and better position. (Business Club)

15. After years of business as usual the newspaper decided it was time to change their Real Estate Classified Sales department and hired four new Sales Executives. I was one of them. I was the only one hired from the outside – everyone else came through internal transfer. We were formed into teams of two. However, after three weeks, my partner, upset with the changes made to her position, left the company. She was to have trained me, and for the next two months I managed my accounts on my own. Having received very little training prior to her departure, and little assistance after she left, I did what I do best: I rolled with the punches and largely trained myself.

My accounts flourished while I taught myself how to place ads and found answers to my questions by developing close relationships with my co-workers. During that transitional time, my manager praised me for picking things up so quickly and for being such a great team player; when I asked her for constructive criticism, she didn't have anything to offer.

The newspaper replaced my former partner and I trained my new one in the manner in which I wish I had been trained. We developed a strong relationship that was the envy of the department, precisely what our manager wanted to achieve when she initially implemented the new changes. Other co-workers could see the strength and respect in our partnership and expressed a disappointment that they didn't have that kind of relationship with their partner as well. Eight months later my partner was recognized as being a key player; she received a promotion and credits me for it. (Newspaper)

16. One lesson I learned the hard way was that the climate set by the person in charge has a direct impact on the morale, commitment and productivity the entire organization. Tension among the staff and members in the light of a new General Manager was both high and continuous. His managerial style and manner of communication was not that to which we had been accustomed. He had come to us from another property within the company. Even though I was one of the youngest of his department heads, I took it upon myself to speak privately with him on more than one occasion.

I felt uncomfortable walking the line between our boss and my colleagues, and developed a plan for how I wanted to conduct the conversation. My Manager and I agreed that I would share the feelings of the department heads while not attributing comments to any particular individual. My approach worked perfectly, and the results were dramatic. Within two months, everyone in the Club, including members, noticed and commented on the visible and sustained improvement in the climate and morale in the Club. I am proud of my initiative, and my willingness to face my fear and proceed. (Business Club)

17. During a university internship, I worked in Alaska for a cruise ship company. Over that nine- month period I worked my way up from cleaning toilets and waiting tables to a supervisory position. Toward the end of my internship, my ship struck a rock in Tracey Arm and began to sink. I kept my calm and did my part to help evacuate the 93 elderly passengers in just 21 minutes. Our entire crew was commended in the national press for having "responded professionally and according to protocol." (Juneau Empire, July 29, 1999) (Cruise Ship Company)

18. Private Events was a separate career track within my company, and was completely separate from my area of Member Relations. Our Club had two Private Events directors, and they did a phenomenal job. However, on one occasion, staffing and coverage between the two of them did not happen and both were off at the same time. When this happened, a scheduled event, worth about $1,000 net, was on the verge of failure. Since many in the Club looked to me for help in times of special need, they brought this situation to me.

   Private Events used their own proprietary software, and Member Relations directors are not cross-trained in its use. However, since I believe in being cross-trained in other areas, and because I was interested and had taken the initiative to learn it, I not only knew their software, I had it installed on my computer. Faced with an immediate need to pull the event together ON-THE-SPOT, I did exactly that. As a result, the Club member had a flawless event, and I saved the Club, the Private Events function, and the individual whose event it was a great deal of embarrassment. (Business Club)

19. Having come from the hourly ranks, I am very aware of the importance of managers paying attention to high-potential employees, and being willing to go to bat for them when necessary. I have been fortunate in having hired employees with aptitudes for greater responsibility, and am committed to facilitating their personal development. One young woman stands out for me. She came in as a front desk clerk and rapidly mastered all aspects of that position. Based on her demonstrated performance, positive member feedback and engaging personality, I followed our procedures to get her onto a fast track to becoming a department head. In less than one year, while working full-time for me, she completed our in-house training program and passed all of her

exams with flying colors and is now a Membership Director. One of the very first people she enrolled as a member was Clay Aiken, and no, they were not friends. (Business Club)

20. Our corporate headquarters had a formal mentoring program that involved all tenured Member Relations Directors. The company hired a young woman right out of college and into the position of Member Relations Director in a Club about 80 miles away from me. I was assigned to mentor her. I knew from first-hand experience that the Company's self-directed training program for certification as a Member Relations Director did not adequately and quickly train a new-hire to pass the exams.

Because I also knew that her Club manager had given her only a six-month window to become certified, I decided to create a custom mentoring program designed to fill the voids I knew from personal experience existed because while working full-time, it took me over a year to pass the exams. While still maintaining my workload, I worked with her diligently on the phone, on both my time and company time, and spent one full weekend working with her at her Club. She passed her exams with flying colors and credits me with her success. Corporate and property general management recognized me for my willingness to go beyond expectations. (Business Club)

21. Based on prior performance, I was selected to update and improve not only our Club's new-hire training program but the accompanying handbook as well. I conducted a gap analysis as I analyzed all aspects of what I went through in the program, and what I read in the handbook, comparing the ideal with what actually took place. Upon completing that process, I recommended updates to the Handbook and the service-

training program. Club Management accepted all of my recommendations and I received both a performance bonus as well as commendations from Club manager. My work enabled future new-hires to receive a more in-depth orientation to the Club, and for the Club to achieve a more rapid return on their training dollars. (Business Club)

22. I completed my university Senior Internship during my Junior year aboard a small cruise ship in Alaska. While working full-time on my ship duties, I completed my senior project, which was the creation from scratch of a comprehensive New-Hire Employee Handbook for use aboard ship, which to the best of my knowledge is still in use. Company management was so impressed with my work and my work ethic that they offered me a management position at the end of my internship. Flattered, I nonetheless declined and returned to complete my degree. (Cruise Ship Company / University)

23. After planning everything to the nth degree, I experienced the BEST THREE DAYS OF MY LIFE – my wedding. From the tiara to the train of my dress to the table arrangements – I planned everything, and had hands-on involvement in most of it as well. Everything within my control went just as I had envisioned it. Why is my wedding an accomplishment for my résumé? Because by utilizing my contacts with the industry and the area, and by doing many things myself, I created an elegant $15,500 wedding for only $8,371, a savings of $6,629. *I promise you that I am just as detail-oriented, cost-conscious and frugal when it comes to spending my employer's money as I am with my own.*

End of SPECIAL SKILLS and ACCOMPLISHMENTS DATA BANKS

Your Fill-In Practice Résumé

- *YOUR NAME*
Your Street Address
Your City, State, and Zip
Your Cell and Home Telephone Numbers
Your E-Mail Address

OBJECTIVE: A full-time, permanent Marketing management position where I will be expected to analyze marketing problems, identify needs, develop and implement creative and profitable solutions, be held accountable for the results, and rewarded accordingly

SPECIAL SKILLS AND ABILITIES

REPRESENTATIVE PROFESSIONAL ACCOMPLISHMENTS
[subcategory]

[subcategory]

[subcategory]

[subcategory]

So. How was that?

My hope is that you had to give a good deal of thought before making decisions about what to leave in and what to leave out.

If you stuck with it, give yourself a pat on the back. You earned it, and you may have a little headache as a result of sorting things out. That's good because it shows you were engaged in the process.

By that very action of putting yourself in her shoes, then thinking and deciding how best to present yourself, you are separating yourself from the mass of your competitors, the ones who put together one single **generic** résumé and lazily shotgun it to all sorts of **specific** positions, and then wonder why their phone does not ring.

Her complete functional résumé follows. You'll notice that she added "**Personal Traits**" to **SPECIAL SKILLS AND ABILITIES**. If you want to do that as well, or prefer to use other words to tell the reader what you bring to the *"world of work,"* please do so.

I encourage you to tailor this process to your needs and your personality, just as I want you to tailor your résumé to each opportunity.

Here is her complete **NARRATIVE** functional résumé. Using an 11 point font, her accomplishments begin half way down the page.

Before you read the résumé, I would like to make a prediction, and I hope I am wrong.

I predict that when you see her résumé, alarm bells will likely go off inside your head when you see that it is more than two pages.

If that is the case, take a couple of deep breaths. Those are your old tapes kicking in, the ones that say you cannot have a résumé more than two pages in length, or that if your résumé looks different, it will be rejected, or… or… or…

Remember: you WANT to stand out, and you cannot do that when your résumé looks just like everyone else's résumé.

Remember too that using the résumé you are about to see, she is still getting calls, even though she is no longer on the market.

Deep breath. Turn the page. **Client's Résumé for Comparison:**

CLIENT'S NAME
Street Address
City, State, and Zip
Telephone Numbers
E-Mail Address

OBJECTIVE: A full-time, permanent Marketing management position where I will be expected to analyze marketing problems, identify needs, develop and implement creative and profitable solutions, be held accountable for the results, and rewarded accordingly

PERSONAL TRAITS, SPECIAL SKILLS AND ABILITIES

Hold high expectations for my performance, strive for high levels of personal achievement

Maintain poise, self-confidence in free-flowing situations; adjust and thrive in new environments

Quick study; able to apply what I have learned and work effectively without supervision

Routinely achieve profit objectives while working within established budgets

Committed to achieving and maintaining consistently high levels of client satisfaction

Confident when faced with learning new software / computer applications

Consensus builder; strong personal influencing skills; rapidly put people at ease, build trust

Take initiative to create pragmatic, effective solutions to business problems

Happy person, committed to both my colleagues and my company

REPRESENTATIVE PROFESSIONAL ACCOMPLISHMENTS

MARKETING CREATIVITY FOR PROFITABILITY, FUNDRAISING AND GOOD WILL

- During my first New Home Open House program, I wondered: *Why do we devote two whole pages to an ineffective map when each home listing is equipped with directions?"* No one could answer that question for me since they'd been doing it that way for a while, so I created an alternative, which the newspaper adopted and still uses to this day. My solution was to group homes located in the same region together to make it easier for the reader to find homes in areas they are interested in; it encouraged the listing agent to offer a web address for more information and it returned the back two pages of the map to the advertising sales staff as additional space they could sell for revenue generation. (Newspaper)

- As Member Relations Director, I managed a number of member committees. The "Women on the Move" committee was one of my most committed and dynamic. Within the company, I know of at least five sister Clubs that have copied my design. It has been a very successful forum for building political and community relations. The relationship of which I am most proud is the one we have established with NATIONAL BOOK STORE. On my initiative, I contacted their regional marketing director and we have formed an ongoing relationship bringing visiting authors to speak at dinner events at the Club. It has been a popular win/win for BOOK STORE, the authors, my members, and the Club. (Business Club)

- Clay Aiken's Foundation approached the Club to partner with them in a fundraiser for charity. We accepted their offer, and I was responsible for marketing the event.

Within one month, we had sold out the event to the maximum capacity of our facility.

Working with his Foundation, I developed marketing pieces, helped design and write ad copy for our newsletter and members' website (both of which I wrote and maintained), developed and implemented an e-mail and poster campaign for the Club, and facilitated an introduction to the local newspaper's Features Editor. This was the first event of this kind we have done and it was a stellar success; over 50 members participated and we raised over $300,000 for his foundation, which enables summer camps for special needs kids (Business Club)

- Harry Potter. Timed with the release of one of the movies, we put on a themed adult/child dinner that included tickets to the movie at the IMAX across the street. We decorated and organized the dining room to look like the Hogwarts dining hall with four long tables based on the four houses in the Harry Potter books. When members came with a child, the child was placed under the Sorting Hat and I had someone with a great voice backstage calling out the names of the Houses, according to where we had seated them for their reservation. The dinner, the room decorations, everything worked to perfection and the members and their children loved it. One member loved it so much that he asked to speak personally with the person who created it – me! When we meet now, he calls me "Harry Potter." He asked me how long I will remain with the Club because Disney needs to pick me up sometime soon! (Business Club)

ACHIEVING PROFITABILITY THROUGH PLANNING

- New to my job, I analyzed my accounts and requested a current run of spending reports. I noticed that several accounts had been spending well over their contracted amount as they advertised with the newspaper. I approached these accounts about signing a new contract at a level equal with their spending. Every one of the six accounts I approached with this option thanked me for my diligence and signed their new and higher contract levels. This resulted in a $40K increase in revenues for my newspaper, and a win-win for the newspaper as well as the client.

  By signing a higher contract level, the newspaper could count on the client achieving this higher level of spending for the next year and the client could count on the newspaper to supply them with lower rates than they had been receiving before. They could advertise more often and still spend the same. One of these accounts had previously been my manager's when she had been a sales person. I encouraged this account to sign at a level which was double what they had done before. They did and both my manager and her manager congratulated me for doing what my manager had been unable to do. (Newspaper)

- As a result of a corporate acquisition and reorganization in January 2007, some of my original Director of Member Relations job duties shifted and I assumed half the responsibilities of a laid-off Private Events director. My new title was Food and Beverage Director of Sales, and I had a $1.5 million sales plan to meet, one that is based on aggressive increases in both food and beverage prices as well as revenue targets. Since there was no marketing plan for this position, the first thing I did upon acquiring this new responsibility was to create and implement a comprehensive one, because up to this point, Private Events had simply relied on word-of-mouth. Four months into the year, we are on track to make plan. (Business Club)

- With only three months experience and only minimal training in my new job, my colleague / peer who was supposed to train me left the club, leaving me as the sole Private Event Director. I met the challenge head-on with a positive attitude tackling it through 13-hour days and six-day work weeks. One colleague commented that she wasn't sure how I managed to do it with a smile on my face every day. I surpassed budget for each month. Period 5 was the largest; The Private Event plan was $118,000; I exceed it by $29,000 with a final total of $149,000. I executed each event perfectly, without dropping a single ball. (Business Club)

- The Member Relations Director position planned and sold events based on what the members were interested in. However, at times I created and hosted events that were off everyone's radar screens, i.e. Chocolate Brunches, dance classes paired with a big dance event, Chocolate and Wine tastings, Scotch tastings and Hurricane Voo-Doo parties to ward off bad hurricanes. Because I was never afraid of trying something new, I constantly sold not just events, but new ideas and change to Club members, my own staff and Club management. I'm proud to say I always received the support I needed to make each new idea a success. (Business Club)

- When my company announced that there would be layoffs in my department, they said they would be making the cuts on the last-in / first-out basis. They called for volunteers and offered a fair package. Since I was the last in, I raised my hand because I just wanted to get on with it. I was astonished and then exceptionally gratified when my managers refused my offer, telling me I was too valuable to be let go and that they had a position for me in the new organization. I believe that says a lot about my productivity and work ethic. (Newspaper)

COURAGE / PERSONAL INITIATIVE

- One lesson I learned the hard way was that the climate set by the person in charge has a direct impact on the morale, commitment and productivity the entire organization. Tension among the staff and members in the light of a new General Manager was both high and continuous. His managerial style and manner of communication was not that to which we had been accustomed.

  He had come to us from another property within the company. Even though I was one of the youngest of his department heads, I took it upon myself to speak privately with him on more than one occasion. I felt uncomfortable walking the line between our boss and my colleagues, and developed a plan for how I wanted to conduct the conversation.

  My Manager and I agreed that I would share the feelings of the department heads while not attributing comments to any particular individual. My approach worked perfectly, and the results were dramatic. Within two months, everyone in the Club, including members, noticed and commented on the visible and sustained improvement in the climate and morale in the Club. I am proud of my initiative, and my willingness to face my fear and proceed. (Business Club)

- During a university internship, I worked in Alaska for a cruise ship company. Over that nine month period I worked my way up from cleaning toilets and waiting tables to a supervisory position. Toward the end of my internship, my ship struck a rock in Tracey Arm and began to sink. I kept my calm and did my part to help evacuate the 93 elderly passengers in just 21 minutes. Our entire crew was commended in the national press for having "responded professionally and according to protocol." (Name of newspaper, July 29, 1999) (Cruise ship company)

MENTORING AND EMPLOYEE DEVELOPMENT

- Our corporate headquarters had a formal mentoring program that involved all tenured Member Relations Directors. The company hired a young woman right out of college and into the position of Member Relations Director in a Club about 80 miles away from me. I was assigned to mentor her. I knew from first-hand experience that the Company's self-directed training program for certification as a Member Relations Director did not adequately and quickly train a new-hire to pass the exams.

Because I also knew that her Club manager had given her only a six-month window to become certified, I decided to create a custom mentoring program designed to fill the voids I knew from personal experience existed because while working full-time, it took me over a year to pass the exams. While still maintaining my workload, I worked with her diligently on the phone, on both my time and company time, and spent one full weekend working with her at her Club. She passed her exams with flying colors and credits me with her success. Corporate and property general management recognized me for my willingness to go beyond expectations. (Business Club)

- I completed my university Senior Internship during my Junior year aboard a small cruise ship in Alaska. While working full-time on my ship duties, I completed my senior project, which was the creation from scratch of a comprehensive New-Hire Employee Handbook for use aboard ship, which to the best of my knowledge is still in use. (Cruise ship company / University)

COST-CONSCIOUS, HANDS-ON CREATIVITY

- After planning everything to the nth degree, I experienced the **_BEST THREE DAYS OF MY LIFE_** – my wedding. From the tiara to the train of my dress to the table arrangements – I planned everything, and had hands-on involvement in most of it as well. Everything within my control went just as I had envisioned it. Why is my wedding an accomplishment for my résumé? Because by utilizing my contacts with the industry and the area, and by doing many things myself, I created an elegant $15,500 wedding for only $8,371, a savings of $6,629. **_I promise you that I am just as detail-oriented and cost-conscious when it comes to spending my employer's money as I am with my own._**

PROFESSIONAL EXPERIENCE:

HER EMPLOYER, CITY, STATE - July 2007 – Present
Real Estate Classified Advertising Sales Executive
Scope of responsibilities:
$1 million sales plan
Direct liaison for over 20 accounts contract levels ranging from $2,500 to $500k
Responsible for account development, recruiting new business and cultivating current business
Responsible for selling print, online, insertions and magazine advertising to all accounts

HER EMPLOYER, PROPERTY LOCATION. CITY, STATE
- May 2001 – July 2007
Member Relations Director - February, 2002 to Date
Manager-in-Training - May, 2001 – February, 2002
Professional Accomplishments: Star Certified: Member Relations Director and Front Desk Attendant
Scope of responsibilities: Manage plethora of activities that increase member retention and food service revenue. Supervise two direct reports.

HER EMPLOYER, CITY, STATE - May - November, 1999
(University Internship)
Promoted to **Relief Lead Customer Service Representative Supervisor -** July – November, 1999
Name, phone number and e-mail address

Customer Service Representative - May – July, 1999
Scope of responsibilities: Supervised eight customer service employees providing range of dining and housekeeping services to an average of 100 passengers per trip from Seattle to Alaska, California and British Columbia

HER HOTEL EMPLOYER, PROPERTY. CITY, STATE - December 1997 - May 1999
Front Desk Shift Leader - October 1998 - May 1999
Front Desk Clerk - December 1997 – October 1998
Professional Accomplishment: Certified **HOTEL** New Hire Trainer
Scope of responsibilities: P&L responsibility for this 302-room property; supervised six

EDUCATION:
UNIVERSITY, School of Hospitality Management (accredited institution) CITY, STATE
Bachelor of Science in Hospitality Management - May, 200l
Minor: Food and Beverage. GPA: 3.0 and Dean's List

COMMUNITY COLLEGE. CITY, STATE December, 1998
Associate of Arts in Hotel and Motel Management   G.P.A:
3.0

OUTSIDE INTERESTS:
- Traveling
- Hiking
- Backpacking
- Boxers
- Horseback riding
- Coordination of themed events
- Cooking and gourmet experimentation

Exercise Comments

OK. You have now gone through the complete process of creating functional résumé in the NARRATIVE format.

You might disagree with the *Special Skills* and *Accomplishments* she included or left in the Data Banks.

You might disagree with the order of presentation.

Perhaps you think the résumé is too long, or the accomplishments are too long. Or not.

Perhaps not because you found yourself getting to know her, and you liked her.

Perhaps you would have created different subcategories.

Whatever your opinions – it's all good because **the only right answer is the one that works for the person.**

There was, however, a thought process.

After thinking about the intended recipients of her letter and résumé, and the impact she wanted to create as they read the documents, she ***intentionally*** decided to present herself as she did.

The key word is "*intentionally*" and that flexibility is the difference between a tailored functional résumé and the more rigidly-structured reverse-chronological résumé.

And as I said, this résumé keeps generating calls, even though she is no longer on the market.

And as I said earlier, ***"Judge by results. Often harsh. Always fair."***

Two Additional Formats

You have now seen a completed NARRATIVE functional résumé. You understand the process of "Selectivity" and are familiar with the other components and the sequence of those components I recommend you follow in the résumé.

Let me show you the two additional formats.

One-Page + Addendum Format

The first is the **ONE-PAGE + ADDENDUM.** It is intended for use when a company demands you submit a one-page résumé.

This format is prepared as a table. Printed on standard 8.5" x 11" paper, it fits on one page. Tightly, but it fits. On her document, she used the header for her contact information.

Since the intent of the functional résumé is to make you stand out in the crowd, like a meatball stands out on a plate of spaghetti, this format will enable you to comply with the company's one-page requirement AND differentiate yourself from your competition.

Much as I would love to claim credit for the brilliance of the **One Page + Addendum** format, I can't. My daughter created it. She has taken what I taught her to a new level. She has given me permission to use her work. It was her résumé you just read.

Here is her **One-Page.** I remind you again that it fits neatly on an 8.5 x 11 sheet of paper.

Objective
A role in which I am expected to analyze problems and needs, develop and implement creative and profitable solutions, and be accountable and rewarded for the results.

Experience
Company / Position
July 2007 to Date. City, State
- $1 million sales plan.
- Direct liaison for over 20 accounts ranging in dollar volume from $10k to $500k.
- Responsible for recruiting new business and selling vast array of products to current business.

Company. May, 2001 – June, 2007
Company/Position – (Promotion). January, 2007 to June, 2007. City, State
- $1.5 million sales plan.
- Salesperson and planner for member and non-member events: weddings, anniversaries, legislative and business related functions.
- Planned / Executed private event direct marketing campaign including creation of collateral materials for Club's Private Dining, Meeting & Wedding planning services.

❖Company/Position – (Promotion.) February, 2002 – January, 2007. City, State
Planned, sold and marketed wide variety of business and social club events to Club's 1300
  Members.
- Basing decisions on what membership asked for, increased Member Events from 40 events per year to 140 per year resulting in positive increase in revenue and increased member satisfaction.
- Responsibilities: Member to Club Liaison, Managed eight, member driven committees; Marketed all Club services via web site and newsletter; Supervised, hired, and trained two, full time front desk concierge agents. Primary responsibility – Member Satisfaction

❖ Company/ Manager-in-Training. May, 2001 – February, 2002. City, State
- First of six admitted to ClubCorp's first Manager-In-Training program - Only FIU student to be accepted
- Trained in: Membership, Food and Beverage, Member Relations, Catering and Kitchen
- Promoted into department head position prior to the end of the program

116

Internships   <u>Florida International University - Community Relations Intern</u>
(Second Internship - Senior Year)

<u>January, 2001 – May, 2001. Florida International University</u>
<u>(FIU) Miami, FL</u>

- Active committee participant: created and executed events hosted by the University. Including Commencement Ceremonies, FIU Miami Film Festival, FIU Food & Wine Extravaganza (A..K.A The South Beach Food & Wine Festival hosted by Food & Wine Magazine)
- Asked by University to remain with the department in an Event Director capacity upon graduation

<u>CruiseWest. Relief Customer Service Supervisor *(Promotion)*</u>
<u>July – November, 1999</u>
<u>CruiseWest. Customer Service Representative - May – July,</u>
<u>1999</u>
<u>CruiseWest. May - November, 1999 *(University Internship)*</u>
<u>Seattle, WA</u>
    • Supervised eight customer service employees providing range of dining and housekeeping services to
        100+ passengers per trip from Seattle to Alaska, California and British Columbia

<u>Marriott Hotels. Front Desk Shift Leader. October, 1998 – May,</u>
<u>1999</u>
<u>Marriott Hotels. Front Desk Clerk. December, 1997 – October,</u>
<u>1998</u>
<u>Miami Dadeland Marriott Hotel (While a Full-time College</u>
<u>Student) December, 1997 – May, 1999</u>

- Certified Marriott New Hire Trainer, P&L responsibility for 302-room property; supervised six

<u>Florida International University. May, 2001. Miami, FL</u>
Education   • B.S., Hospitality Management - 3.0 G.P.A and Dean's List (accredited institution).
<u>Miami-Dade Community College. December, 1998. Miami, FL</u>
- Associate of Arts in Hotel and Motel Management   G.P.A: 3.0

- Traveling & hiking
Interests   • Personal growth seminars: Rich Dad Poor Dad Goal Setting Seminar and Real Estate Investing Seminars (all self-financed)
- Personal Interest in Real Estate – Own and Manage one Investment Property
- Various software: website content creation, proficient and self-taught in Microsoft Word, Excel, PowerPoint and On-Line Services

There you have the essentials, packed onto just one page. If that's all a company wants, they have it.

She devoted a good deal of space to "Internships" because they were unique experiences for her and help set her apart.

How would you use the space? Special certifications? Military experience? Professional affiliations? Special licenses?

Remember, one of the purposes of an effective résumé is to show as many relevant facets of you as there are, until such time as you can speak for yourself.

The **One-Page** contains a lot of information, but my daughter is an over-achiever and one page can only convey so much. She goes above-and-beyond in all that she does, and she created a brilliant twist – she calls it a **One Page + Addendum.**

With the **One-Page**, she is in compliance with the mandate for a one-page document.

✒* With the Addendum, she is simply providing additional information; the company is free to consider it or discard it.

Clever. Inventive. Shows initiative. An astute reader will learn something important about her character.

The **Addendum** contains the same SPECIAL SKILLS AND ABILITIES as well as the same REPRESENTATIVE PROFESSIONAL ACCOMPLISHMENTS as presented in the **Narrative** format.

💣 What makes the Addendum format so unique is the inclusion of the two paragraphs immediately preceding the SPECIAL SKILLS table.

💣 Please note the gentle phrasing of the first paragraph in which she acknowledges the one-page requirement and then politely explains why she went beyond it.

💣 The second paragraph is a free-form opportunity to tell the reader something important about herself, her values and work ethic. Not a lot. Just an interesting taste.

For your purposes, think about a critical piece of information you want the potential employer to know about you – something unique that will make you the meatball.

The approach is powerful and she has used it effectively.

💣 If you are considering using the One-Page + ADDENDUM format, two points of caution:

💣 1. For the first two paragraphs, use no more than one-and-a-half inches of space;

💣 2. For the SPECIAL SKILLS AND ABILITIES table, use no more than three inches. Make certain you will have at least the last three inches of the printable space on that page to get into the REPRESENTATIVE PROFESSIONAL ACCOMPLISHMENTS.

Here is the complete **ONE-PAGE + ADDENDUM**

ALL CONTACT INFORMATION PRESENTED IN THE HEADER

Objective
A role in which I am expected to analyze problems and needs, develop and implement creative and profitable solutions, and be accountable and rewarded for the results.

Experience
Company / Position
July 2007 to Date. City, State
- $1 million sales plan.
- Direct liaison for over 20 accounts ranging in dollar volume from $10k to $500k.
- Responsible for recruiting new business and selling vast array of products to current business.

Company. May, 2001 – June, 2007
Company/Position – (Promotion). January, 2007 to June, 2007. City, State
- $1.5 million sales plan.
- Salesperson and planner for member and non-member events: weddings, anniversaries, legislative and business related functions.
- Planned / Executed private event direct marketing campaign including creation of collateral materials for Club's Private Dining, Meeting & Wedding planning services.

❖Company/Position – (Promotion.) February, 2002 – January, 2007. City, State
Planned, sold and marketed wide variety of business and social club events to Club's 1300
   Members.
- Basing decisions on what membership asked for, increased Member Events from 40 events per year to 140 per year resulting in positive increase in revenue and increased member satisfaction.
- Responsibilities: Member to Club Liaison, Managed eight, member driven committees; Marketed all Club services via web site and newsletter; Supervised, hired, and trained two, full time front desk concierge agents. Primary responsibility – Member Satisfaction

❖ Company/ Manager-in-Training. May, 2001 – February, 2002. City, State
- First of six admitted to ClubCorp's first Manager-In-Training program - Only FIU student to be accepted
- Trained in: Membership, Food and Beverage, Member Relations, Catering and Kitchen
- Promoted into department head position prior to the end of the program

Internships
Florida International University - Community Relations Intern
(Second Internship - Senior Year)

120

January, 2001 – May, 2001. Florida International University (FIU) Miami, FL

- Active committee participant: created and executed events hosted by the University. Including Commencement Ceremonies, FIU Miami Film Festival, FIU Food & Wine Extravaganza (A..K.A The South Beach Food & Wine Festival hosted by Food & Wine Magazine)
- Asked by University to remain with the department in an Event Director capacity upon graduation

CruiseWest. Relief Customer Service Supervisor *(Promotion)* July – November, 1999
CruiseWest. Customer Service Representative - May – July, 1999
CruiseWest. May - November, 1999 *(University Internship)* Seattle, WA

- Supervised eight customer service employees providing range of dining and housekeeping services to
    100+ passengers per trip from Seattle to Alaska, California and British Columbia

Marriott Hotels. Front Desk Shift Leader. October, 1998 – May, 1999
Marriott Hotels. Front Desk Clerk. December, 1997 – October, 1998
Miami Dadeland Marriott Hotel (While a Full-time College Student) December, 1997 – May, 1999

- Certified Marriott New Hire Trainer, P&L responsibility for 302-room property; supervised six

Florida International University. May, 2001. Miami, FL

Education

- B.S., Hospitality Management - 3.0 G.P.A and Dean's List (accredited institution).

Miami-Dade Community College. December, 1998. Miami, FL

- Associate of Arts in Hotel and Motel Management   G.P.A: 3.0

Interests

- Traveling & hiking
- Personal growth seminars: Rich Dad Poor Dad Goal Setting Seminar and Real Estate Investing Seminars (all self-financed)
- Personal Interest in Real Estate – Own and Manage one Investment Property
- Various software: website content creation, proficient and self-taught in Microsoft Word, Excel, PowerPoint and On-Line Services

ADDENDUM: NAME, TELEPHONE, EMAIL ADDRESS

This is an addendum to my résumé. A single page résumé shows the reader only a fraction of the candidate's skills and experience. For my job search, I have created data bases of my most relevant **Personal Traits, Special Skills and Abilities**, and my most significant **Representative Professional Accomplishments**. The ones that follow most closely coincide with your position requirements.

This is what I have learned: My post-college work with both the *NEWSPAPER* and the BUSINESS CLUB has taught me that I am here to make a difference by making improvements. I am not here to maintain the status quo. At first, coming out of an hourly job into my first salaried position, I did not realize I could improve upon current procedures if I saw a way to make work processes more effective or efficient. Once I realized I could, I took the initiative and I made changes, which resulted in a more effective use of time and money for co-workers and for the bottom line as well.

PERSONAL TRAITS, SPECIAL SKILLS AND ABILITIES

Hold high expectations for my performance, strive for high levels of personal achievement

Maintain poise, self-confidence in free-flowing situations; adjust and thrive in new environments

Quick study; able to apply what I have learned and work effectively without supervision

Routinely achieve profit objectives while working within established budgets

Committed to achieving and maintaining consistently high levels of client satisfaction

Confident when faced with learning new software / computer applications

Consensus builder; strong personal influencing skills; rapidly put people at ease and build trust	Take initiative to create pragmatic, effective solutions to business problems	Happy person, committed to both my colleagues and my company

REPRESENTATIVE PROFESSIONAL ACCOMPLISHMENTS

MARKETING CREATIVITY FOR PROFITABILITY, FUNDRAISING AND GOOD WILL

- During my first New Home Open House program, I wondered: *Why do we devote two whole pages to an ineffective map when each home listing is equipped with directions?"* No one could answer that question for me since they'd been doing it that way for a while, so I created an alternative, which the newspaper adopted and still uses to this day. My solution was to group homes located in the same region together to make it easier for the reader to find homes in areas they are interested in; it encouraged the listing agent to offer a web address for more information and it returned the back two pages of the map to the advertising sales staff as additional space they could sell for revenue generation. (Newspaper)

- As Member Relations Director, I managed a number of member committees. The "Women on the Move" committee was one of my most committed and dynamic. Within the company, I know of at least five sister Clubs that have copied my design. It has been a very successful forum for building political and community relations. The relationship of which I am most proud is the one we have established with NATIONAL BOOK STORE. On my initiative, I contacted their regional marketing director and we have formed an ongoing relationship bringing visiting authors to speak at dinner events at the Club. It has been a popular win/win for BOOK STORE, the authors, my members, and the Club. (Business Club)

- Clay Aiken's Foundation approached the Club to partner with them in a fundraiser for charity. We accepted their offer, and I was responsible for marketing the event. Within one month, we had sold out the event to the maximum capacity of our facility.

  Working with his Foundation, I developed marketing pieces, helped design and write ad copy for our newsletter and members' website (both of which I wrote and maintained), developed and implemented an e-mail and poster campaign for the Club, and facilitated an introduction to the local newspaper's Features Editor. This was the first event of this kind we have done and it was a stellar success; over 50 members participated and we raised over $300,000 for his foundation, which enables summer camps for special needs kids (Business Club)

- Harry Potter. Timed with the release of one of the movies, we put on a themed adult/child dinner that included tickets to the movie at the IMAX across the street. We decorated and organized the dining room to look like the Hogwarts dining hall with four long tables based on the four houses in the Harry Potter books. When members came with a child, the child was placed under the Sorting Hat and I had someone with a great voice backstage calling out the names of the Houses, according to where we had seated them for their reservation. The dinner, the room decorations, everything worked to perfection and the members and their children loved it. One member loved it so much that he asked to speak personally with the person who created it – me! When we meet now, he calls me "Harry Potter."   He asked me how long I will remain with the Club because Disney needs to pick me up sometime soon! (Business Club)

ACHIEVING PROFITABILITY THROUGH PLANNING

- New to my job, I analyzed my accounts and requested a current run of spending reports. I noticed that several accounts had been spending well over their contracted amount as they advertised with the newspaper. I approached these accounts about signing a new contract at a level equal with their spending. Every one of the six accounts I approached with this option thanked me for my diligence and signed their new and higher contract levels. This resulted in a $40K increase in revenues for my newspaper, and a win-win for the newspaper as well as the client.

  By signing a higher contract level, the newspaper could count on the client achieving this higher level of spending for the next year and the client could count on the newspaper to supply them with lower rates than they had been receiving before. They could advertise more often and still spend the same. One of these accounts had previously been my manager's when she had been a sales person. I encouraged this account to sign at a level which was double what they had done before. They did and both my manager and her manager congratulated me for doing what my manager had been unable to do. (Newspaper)

- As a result of a corporate acquisition and reorganization in January 2007, some of my original Director of Member Relations job duties shifted and I assumed half the responsibilities of a laid-off Private Events director. My new title was Food and Beverage Director of Sales, and I had a $1.5 million sales plan to meet, one that is based on aggressive increases in both food and beverage prices as well as revenue targets. Since there was no marketing plan for this position, the first thing I did upon acquiring this new responsibility was to create and implement a comprehensive one, because up to this point, Private Events had simply relied on word-of-mouth. Four months into the year, we are on track to make plan. (Business Club)

- With only three months experience and only minimal training in my new job, my colleague / peer who was supposed to train me left the club, leaving me as the sole Private Event Director. I met the challenge head-on with a positive attitude tackling it through 13-hour days and six-day work weeks. One colleague commented that she wasn't sure how I managed to do it with a smile on my face every day. I surpassed budget for each month. Period 5 was the largest; The Private Event plan was $118,000; I exceed it by $29,000 with a final total of $149,000. I executed each event perfectly, without dropping a single ball. (Business Club)

- The Member Relations Director position planned and sold events based on what the members were interested in. However, at times I created and hosted events that were off everyone's radar screens, i.e. Chocolate Brunches, dance classes paired with a big dance event, Chocolate and Wine tastings, Scotch tastings and Hurricane Voo-Doo parties to ward off bad hurricanes. Because I was never afraid of trying something new, I constantly sold not just events, but new ideas and change to Club members, my own staff and Club management. I'm proud to say I always received the support I needed to make each new idea a success. (Business Club)

126

- When my company announced that there would be layoffs in my department, they said they would be making the cuts on the last-in / first-out basis. They called for volunteers and offered a fair package. Since I was the last in, I raised my hand because I just wanted to get on with it. I was astonished and then exceptionally gratified when my managers refused my offer, telling me I was too valuable to be let go and that they had a position for me in the new organization. I believe that says a lot about my productivity and work ethic. (Newspaper)

COURAGE / PERSONAL INITIATIVE

- One lesson I learned the hard way was that the climate set by the person in charge has a direct impact on the morale, commitment and productivity the entire organization. Tension among the staff and members in the light of a new General Manager was both high and continuous. His managerial style and manner of communication was not that to which we had been accustomed.

  He had come to us from another property within the company. Even though I was one of the youngest of his department heads, I took it upon myself to speak privately with him on more than one occasion. I felt uncomfortable walking the line between our boss and my colleagues, and developed a plan for how I wanted to conduct the conversation. My Manager and I agreed that I would share the feelings of the department heads while not attributing comments to any particular individual.

  My approach worked perfectly, and the results were dramatic. Within two months, everyone in the Club, including members, noticed and commented on the visible and sustained improvement in the climate and morale in the Club. I am proud of my initiative, and my willingness to face my fear and proceed. (Business Club)

- During a university internship, I worked in Alaska for a cruise ship company. Over that nine month period I worked my way up from cleaning toilets and waiting tables to a supervisory position. Toward the end of my internship, my ship struck a rock in Tracey Arm and began to sink. I kept my calm and did my part to help evacuate the 93 elderly passengers in just 21 minutes. Our entire crew was commended in the national press for having "responded professionally and according to protocol." (Name of newspaper, July 29, 1999) (Cruise ship company)

MENTORING AND EMPLOYEE DEVELOPMENT

- Our corporate headquarters had a formal mentoring program that involved all tenured Member Relations Directors. The company hired a young woman right out of college and into the position of Member Relations Director in a Club about 80 miles away from me. I was assigned to mentor her. I knew from first-hand experience that the Company's self-directed training program for certification as a Member Relations Director did not adequately and quickly train a new-hire to pass the exams. Because I also knew that her Club manager had given her only a six-month window to become certified, I decided to create a custom mentoring program designed to fill the voids I knew from personal experience existed because while working full-time, it took me over a year to pass the exams.

While still maintaining my workload, I worked with her diligently on the phone, on both my time and company time, and spent one full weekend working with her at her Club. She passed her exams with flying colors and credits me with her success. Corporate and property general management recognized me for my willingness to go beyond expectations. (Business Club)

- I completed my university Senior Internship during my Junior year aboard a small cruise ship in Alaska. While working full-time on my ship duties, I completed my senior project, which was the creation from scratch of a comprehensive New-Hire Employee Handbook for use aboard ship, which to the best of my knowledge is still in use. (Cruise ship company / University)

COST-CONSCIOUS, HANDS-ON CREATIVITY

- After planning everything to the nth degree, I experienced the *BEST THREE DAYS OF MY LIFE* – my wedding. From the tiara to the train of my dress to the table arrangements – I planned everything, and had hands-on involvement in most of it as well. Everything within my control went just as I had envisioned it. Why is my wedding an accomplishment for my résumé? Because by utilizing my contacts with the industry and the area, and by doing many things myself, I created an elegant $15,500 wedding for only $8,371, a savings of $6,629. *I promise you that I am just as detail-oriented and cost-conscious when it comes to spending my employer's money as I am with my own.*

PROFESSIONAL EXPERIENCE:

HER EMPLOYER, CITY, STATE. July, 2007 – Present
Real Estate Classified Advertising Sales Executive
Scope of responsibilities:
$1 million sales plan
Direct liaison for over 20 accounts contract levels ranging from $2,500 to $500k

Responsible for account development, recruiting new business and cultivating current business
Responsible for selling print, online, insertions and magazine advertising to all accounts

HER EMPLOYER, PROPERTY LOCATION. CITY, STATE - May 2001 – July 2007
Member Relations Director - February, 2002 to Date
Manager-in-Training - May, 2001 – February, 2002
Professional Accomplishments: Star Certified: Member Relations Director and Front Desk Attendant
Scope of responsibilities: Manage plethora of activities that increase member retention and food service revenue. Supervise two direct reports.

HER EMPLOYER, CITY, STATE - May - November, 1999 *(University Internship)*
Promoted to **Relief Lead Customer Service Representative Supervisor** - July – November, 1999
Name, phone number and e-mail address

Customer Service Representative - May – July, 1999
Scope of responsibilities: Supervised eight customer service employees providing range of dining and housekeeping services to an average of 100 passengers per trip from Seattle to Alaska, California and British Columbia
HER HOTEL EMPLOYER, PROPERTY. CITY, STATE - December 1997 - May 1999
Front Desk Shift Leader - October 1998 - May 1999
Front Desk Clerk - December 1997 – October 1998
Professional Accomplishment: Certified **HOTEL** New Hire Trainer
Scope of responsibilities: P&L responsibility for this 302-room property; supervised six

EDUCATION:
UNIVERSITY, School of Hospitality Management (accredited institution) CITY, STATE
Bachelor of Science in Hospitality Management - May, 2001
Minor: Food and Beverage. GPA: 3.0 and Dean's List

HER Community College. CITY, STATE December, 1998
Associate of Arts in Hotel and Motel Management   G.P.A: 3.0

OUTSIDE INTERESTS:
Traveling, hiking, backpacking, Boxers, horseback riding
Coordination of themed events
Cooking and gourmet experimentation

End of *ONE-PAGE + ADDENDUM*

And there you have the second of three functional résumé formats.

Technical + Narrative Format

Here is the third variation. Like the **Addendum** format, I cannot take credit for it. My son combined my **Narrative** format with one he learned from a colleague and modified it for his technology-based job search when he got out of the Navy.

This format makes it very easy to immediately know, at a glance, what expertise the applicant has in terms of hardware, software, operating systems, database management, systems administration and the like.

As with the other two formats, this one works fine with standard font sizes and regular paper.

Out of a field of over 50 applicants, my son used this résumé to secure a position as systems engineer at a prestigious engineering university.

It would have been much easier for him to have simply listed job duties and responsibilities, rather than wrestle with **accomplishments.** We spent a lot of time asking and answering the question, *"SO WHAT?"* until we transformed his "activities" into "accomplishments."

As you read the résumé, you may notice that my son does not have a degree. While I cannot prove it, I believe that it was his orientation to results and his willingness to present himself in terms of what he had *accomplished* in the Navy and civilian jobs that set him apart from the other applicants, (most of whom had degrees), and enabled him to win the position.

Perhaps you would like to give some thought to the implications of that last paragraph?

Specialized Industry Knowledge:
Computer and Information Technology, Defense and Federal Systems

Operating Systems Expertise
Windows - XP Pro, 2000, NT, ME, 98, 95, Workgroups, DOS, UNIX(HP-UX 10.20)

Hardware Expertise
DELL, Compaq, Hewlett-Packard, Digital, IBM PCs, Laptops, and compatibles, PDAs, RAID, XYLAN/Alcatel, Cisco Switches, 3COM, SCSI, Scanners, Printers, CD/DVD RW Drives, Jaz, Zip, Tape Drives, Digital Cameras, Smart Phones, PKI

Software Expertise
Adobe PhotoShop, IE 7 and previous versions, Ghost, Microsoft Office Professional 2007 and previous versions, MS Exchange 5.5, WordPerfect, MS FrontPage, VISIO, Netscape, Norton (AntiVirus, CleanSweep, Ghost), McAffee, Norton Internet Security, SpyBot, AVG, WinZip, TeamViewer

Database Expertise
MS Access, Centuras SQLBase

Network Protocol Expertise:
DNS, DHCP, Ethernet, FastEthernet, Fiber, Token Ring, IIS, IP, WINS, TCP/IP, Wi-Fi

Network Management Expertise:

NAME/Address/Telephone/Email

Objective: UNIVERSITY Systems Engineer / Network Administrator

Overview of Professional Experience

Top-Secret and SCI clearance since 10/00 through US Navy and authorized access to Federal Bureau of Investigation (FBI) 01/02 – 07/06. Ten years experience in these areas: managing, configuring, upgrading, adds/moves/changes to LANs/WANs, servers, PCs, and laptops. Level I & Level II desk-side/phone/remote support, troubleshooting Network systems design, implementation, and administration. Effectively manage and maintain equipment worth millions of dollars

Relevant Professional Experience:

NETWORK SET-UP & MANAGEMENT:

Administrator on GOVERNMENT AGENCY'S Secret network operating on W2K and Unclassified network running XP Pro.

One of five techs to install 130+ Compaq workstations, HP printers and scanners and over 100 P.O.S. (Point Of Sales) Partech systems on the

Network Administration, Network OS Installation and Upgrades, Network Security

Systems Administration Expertise:
2003/2000/NT 4.0 Server Administration – add/delete/modify accounts, user rights/limits/passwords, tape backups/restores. Exchange Server 5.5 Administration – add/delete/modify accounts, user rights/limits/passwords, tape backups/restores. Software and Server OS Installations and Upgrades. Systems Troubleshooting. Systems Storage Management. Security Risk Management Network Software Installations.

Network Support Expertise:
Support Desktop Systems Configurations and Troubleshooting, Expert Support Problem Resolution, Very Strong Positive Customer Support and Team Player

Web, Application & Messaging Servers Expertise: MS Exchange 5.5, FrontPage 2000, and 2002, 2003, LanChat, Game Server, MP3 Server

Windows 2000 platform in an allotted one month time frame without errors

Member of team that set up over 20,000 FBI Dell workstations, 2,400 printers, 1,200 scanners (including multifunction printer/scanner/copier/fax), 1,300 Cisco Switches, and over 1,200 Cisco Routers. All accomplished on time, on budget and without error

Implemented relocation of eight servers on two networks using TCP/IP communications with an Ethernet backbone on a Windows NT 4.0 platform. 24/7 user support

Utilized Top Secret/SCI Clearance to provide desk-side & phone support to users running Windows NT 4.0 workstation. Completed NT administration functions; adds/moves/changes including assisting the replacement of well over 1500 Dell and HP workstations; installing NT4.0 and all civilian and government applications to Navy standards; documented PCs, printers, scanners; assisted in the offload of old PCs to DRMS (Defense Reutilization and Marketing Service)

135

Personally responsible for 2 networked medical and dental programs SNAP (System Non-tactical Allocated Program) Allocated Medical System (SAMS) and Dental Management Information System (DENMIS) consisting of 9 workstations and the main database on a Compaq Rack Mounted Server.

Accountable for configuration, installation, and maintenance of software, management of users, and globally the main point of contact for customer support. Directly responsible for successfully upgrading the program from DOS based to Windows 32- bit in minimal down time

DATA MIGRATION:

Migrated GOVERNMENT AGENCY'S existing field offices and smaller remote sites from a token ring Novell network base infrastructure to a scalable fiber Ethernet infrastructure that supports their current capacity and beyond

SYSTEM UPGRADES:

Implementation team member for - replacement of over 5,000 3-Com 905 NICs with 990 NICs. Ran CAT5 and Fiber drops for the US Navy and GOVERNMENT AGENCY

Independently reloaded an entirely new ATIS Server (Networked TAG RAID Database and a 7-Bay CD-ROM) on a Digital Polaris ZX 6000 Series SCSI Server. Installed Windows NT Server 4.0, Centura's SQLBase Server 6.1.2-PTF4, MS Office 97 suite and Microsoft Service Pack 3

Independently installed and configured NETg training software on UNCLASS network, which consisted of over 30

CD's. Trained co-workers on the management of the software and user database

Disassembled a 9 slot XYLAN Switch with over 100 CAT 5 cables and 10 fiber connections for maintenance and reassembled in minimal downtime

Provided special project coordination and implementation of software and operating system upgrades, and assisted groups with migrating and testing new software to support their individual needs. Involved in the deployment of, and provided support for, the following applications: MS Office, Microsoft Outlook, Internet Explorer, Netscape, WinZip, which I have installed on end-user's workstations

STAFF TRAINING:

Trained over 150 appointed GOVERNMENT AGENCY employees in group and individual sessions to become proficient as PKI RAs (Registration Authority) in the allotted time

Trained over 40 GOVERNMENT AGENCY Computer Specialists on their startup and installation scripts and how to reclone their workstations, enabling all users to learn and apply uniform applications and procedures to effectively use new Dell systems. Completed all training within budgeted time frame

Developed and implemented training for over 30 Navy co-workers by group and individual sessions on installation of the software, management of users, proper backups and restores, and fixes for common system configuration issues
Developed and implemented training for over 50 Navy co-workers in the use and administration of the network to include NT4.0 server farm integration and basic network

troubleshooting tips through the writing and presentation of lectures and briefs

DATA MANAGEMENT:

Managed Ship's supplies and parts database on an HP-UX 10.20 OS (SNAP) used by the entire ship of 800+ clients

CUSTOMER INTERFACE:

Managed user rights, network and server access, and mail box limits on all three Classified and Unclassified networks, comprised of 25 servers and more than 1,000 workstations running various operation systems while serving on USS Blue Ridge (Communications Ship and personal vessel of the Pacific Fleet US Admiral)

Provided full-time, 24/7 support to users, including: network/server support Windows NT. 4.0 platform; on-site desktop support for PCs with Windows 95/98/NT4.0/2000 operating systems and continuous on-site support for Applications, Printers, Scanners, CD R/W drives, NICs

• As NT Administrator, stood day and night shifts on board ship and on shore in Japan. **Day duties:** consisted of taking trouble calls, entering them into an MS Access database trouble log, resolving user hardware, software or network problems, or escalating as necessary and providing Level I and II (telephone) support, or Level III on-site support. Provided excellent customer service: created/deleted/ modified user accounts and email accounts, resolved wide range of trouble calls including faulty hardware problems, missing or corrupt files, training users how to use their workstation, applications and connecting hardware. **Night duties**: ran system backups, weekly network reboots, maintained action log of actions/alarms/situations, answered trouble calls, handled any open trouble calls the day shift were unable to complete, downloaded up-to-date virus updates, uploaded them to the servers and pushed them out to every workstation

PROFESSIONAL HISTORY:

TECHNICAL CONTRACT COMPANY, Federal Group – Senior Systems Engineer – 9/2004 – 7/2006
GOVERNMENT AGENCY ITS Support Contractor: 9/2005 – 7/2006 (completion)
Solely responsible for the Denver Field Office and all eighteen surrounding Colorado and Wyoming offices as the support for the local ITS (Information Technology Specialist)

Administrators. Provide the ITSs with troubleshoot training techniques prior to and/or when problems arise. Voluntarily created batch scripts that simplified tasks which notably saved them time and money.

GOVERNMENT AGENCY *PKI Deployment*: Contract duration *9/2004 – 7/2005* (completion)
In a team of 4, traveled to 26 major US GOVERNMENT AGENCY field offices/cities in a 10 month span as a RM (Registration Manager) to register all personnel in each office, install card readers, volunteered to train appointed individuals to become RAs (Registration Authorities - PKI Administrator) in each office totaling over 150 Admins, and without being asked, created simple step-by-step procedures for the RAs to follow which the GOVERNMENT AGENCY uses as a modified standard GOVERNMENT AGENCY-wide.
Reason for Leaving: Contract completed 7/2006, no contracts followed

TECHNICAL CONTRACT COMPANY –CRUISE SHIP CLIENT – Contract duration: 6/2003 – 7/2003

One of five chosen to travel to Monfalcone, Italy to install P.O.S. Systems, Compaq workstations, HP scanners, digital scanners, printers, network printers, multi-function printers and BOCA printers throughout CRUISE SHIP CLIENT'S newest ship, the Glory. All competed within the allotted one month time frame without errors.
Reason for Leaving: Contract and installation completed

TECHNICAL CONTRACTS COMPANY. *–GOVERNMENT AGENCY CLIENT – Contract duration: 1/2002 – 3/2003 & 8/2003 – 6/2004*
Team member and batch scripts writer on GOVERNMENT AGENCY'S XMXMX Project installation team traveling nationwide to upgrade GOVERNMENT AGENCY'S networks, servers, and desktop PCs. Direct- responsibility for creating install scripts for ITs to run on each site's workstations
Reason for Leaving 3/2003: Downsized when GOVERNMENT AGENCY was forced to make budget cuts
Reason for Leaving 6/2004: Contract completed 4/2004, no contracts followed

Network Systems Administrator / Technician
US Navy, 9/1998 – 9/2001. Rank: E-4. Honorable discharge.
Served our country as a Network / Systems Administrator / Technician (multi-purpose) on board the only Communications Ship in the Pacific Ocean, USS Blue Ridge (LCC 19), Yokosuka, Japan. Responsible for managing three networks, each with a different security classification: Unclassified, Secret, SCI/Top Secret.
Reason for Leaving: Completed enlistment commitment

CERTIFICATIONS AND EDUCATION:
DCSE (Dell Certified System Expert) 1999
Information Systems Technology (IT) "A" School. US Navy. Great Lakes, IL. 1997

Security Clearance: Top Secret/SCI currently in OPR. Initially awarded October, 2000 through Department of Defense

REFERENCES:
Provided as appropriate

~ **End of *TECHNICAL + NARRATIVE* ~**

Recapping Sample Functional Résumés

Well, we are pretty much as the end of our functional résumé rope.

In this section, you have had the opportunity to practice using Data Bases in the "Selectivity" exercise around Special Skills and Abilities and Representative Professional Accomplishments and then compared your selections with a successful résumé.

You have learned how to construct the three basic functional résumé formats:

• Narrative
• One-Page + Addendum
• Technical + Narrative

I believe you now have the tools to kick your job search up to the next level and make your phone ring with a recruiter on the other end of the line.

But before you do, I'd be sorry to see you apply **the same old "spaghetti" cover letters** and **job search strategies** with your brand new, cool and unique **stand-out-like-a-*"MEATBALL"* résumés.**

So, please proceed to the Bonus Section, my parting gift to you.

Bonus Section

Stand Out!

- **Targeted Cover Letters**
- **Exploratory Cover Letters**
- **Job Search Strategies**
- **Four Magic Sentences**

Using Your New Résumé in Ways that Make You Stand Out

When clients read their new functional résumé the first time, they are frequently stunned and amazed at all they have accomplished. I love it when their eyes light up, or sometimes go misty, and they ask, "Who *is* this person?"

I hope you have that same experience.

You now have everything you need to create your own functional résumé. I've fulfilled my part of the deal, and the next step, writing your résumé and then using it effectively, is up to you.

As my parting gift to you, I'd like to offer some suggestions and strategies for using your new resume. They've worked very effectively for me and for others as well.

There's no sense to having gone to all this effort if you are going to use your new tool in the same old ways.

Introduction to Cover Letters

For years I kept a collection of the most ludicrous, ineffective, embarrassing and downright funny cover letters I received and kept them in a file called, *"WHAT? Are You Kidding Me?!"* But somewhere along the way, it went away.

Going back thirty years, I can still recall the best three of the bunch.

My favorite was a typed letter from a minister who sold a full range of insurance products on the side.

Right in the first paragraph, he told me his last name was Bishop and told me, and I quote, *"You can call me Bish."*

"Bish" had prepared a neatly-typed letter in which he provided a detailed list of everything he expected the company to do for him, once we hired him.

The list was extensive, and he amplified it with precisely-drawn lines going to empty spaces all over the page. In very meticulous printing, he added probably 15 additional expectations and explanations.

His letter made a lasting impression on me, but not a good one and I didn't call him.

The second letter was from an experienced sales representative. His letter slipped over onto page two and contained a good deal of relevant information.

As I got to page two, I was getting more and more interested in what he had to say. That is, until he ended the letter telling me in no uncertain terms that the only way he would consider accepting an offer would be if we agreed, in writing, to let him bring his wife on all trips, fly them both First Class, put them up only in premier hotels and pay them each a daily stipend of $1,000.

Thank you, noooo.

The third letter came from a young woman just out of college. Evidentially someone had advised her that flattery was the absolute best way to get an interview.

She dedicated all but the final paragraph to praising my employer up one wall and down the other. I would have been honored to work for the company she said we were.

According to her, we were a leading force of social change in the community (which we absolutely were not), that our customer service was legendary (which it absolutely was not), and that we were a significant global presence (which made me laugh as we were just starting to think beyond our time zone.) She closed with an impassioned plea to give her the honor of working with such a wonderful organization.

In due time, all three applicants received a TBNT letter.

I know that those three are extremes, and that you would never jeopardize a potential opportunity with such silliness.

Nonetheless, silliness happens, as they say.

Elements of Targeted Cover Letters

This three-part format has worked well for me and for others. I urge you to consider using it yourself.

As with the résumé samples, it fits fine on a standard 8.5 x 11 sheet of paper

With record levels of unemployment and stacks of résumés to read, recruiters and interviewers are busy people. Their eyes can only take so much, so don't waste their time with platitudes and air-words. Get to the point. Give them what they need.

Part One:

In a couple of short sentences, tell the recipient the position for which you are applying, the date of the notice, and where you saw it.

Part Two:

Since you will have already become familiar with the key requirements of the position and know you are a good match before you submit your résumé, create a two-column *"Parallel Assessment"* table.

Give the left column the heading "**YOU SEEK**" and using bullet points, summarize the three to five most critical requirements for the position.

Since you are applying for a position where your qualifications match their requirements, title the right column, "**I OFFER**". Then provide a bullet-pointed parallel assessment of how you match their key requirements, thus showing yourself as the solution to their needs.

Part Three:

Even though your phone number is on your résumé and letterhead, repeat it in the closing and tell them you will follow up with them in X number of days. Seven business days seems like an appropriate time frame to me. Make sure you honor your word.

Please turn the page for a **sample cover letter**. Again, it too will fit nicely on one 8.5 x 11 sheet of stationary.

Date
Name
Position
Company
Address
City, Sate, Zip

Dear Mr. Jones,

I am responding to your March 29th posting on your website for a marketing manager to manage your Classified Department.

Based on the requirements covered in the job posting, I believe I am about a 95% ideal match for the position.

You Seek:	*I Offer:*
1. Ten years experience profitably managing staff of seven classified ad specialists during this recession. Position requires deft hand in providing client-focused customer service while maintaining profitability	• Nine years of ever-more-complex managerial and sales experience. In NEWSPAPER, I increased classified ad revenues by 7% in this terrible economy. In BUSINESS CLUB, I exceeded both retention and membership targets by 8%
2. Ability to deal simultaneously with multiple accounts	• Sold ad space to over 20 accounts and increased Club membership by 16%
3. Professionally deal with customers in environment of pressure and tight deadlines	• Have earned reputation as being able to defuse conflict, keeping both my cool and the clients, and getting the job done

4. Track record of hitting or exceeding targets and managing within operating budget	• Based on my results and abilities, I have a history of asking my manager to increase my targets. Because of my results, when my company downsized, they adjusted their layoff policy to retain me

Thank you for reviewing my credentials. I can be reached at 000.123.4567. If I do not hear from you in seven business days, I'll call you on **DATE** to be sure you received this letter.

Sincerely,

Your Name
Address
Telephone and E-mail

So. There you have my cover letter for responding to a specific position.

Strategy for Exploratory Letters for Mass Mailing

While I would prefer you follow the process I have outlined earlier and apply for specific positions rather than doing an exploratory mailing campaign, I know there will be occasions when you will need to do a mass mailing, like to search firms.

♦※ When you do, I suggest you follow the two-column format of the preceding letter. In addition, make certain you continue to keep the focus on what YOU can do for others, *not* on what you want them to do for you.

Here is a strategy for doing just that.

In many major cities, there is a weekly business newspaper that generally contains "*Business Journal*" in its' name. Please see http://www.bizjournals.com.

Generally, each week a business journal publishes a comprehensive and well-researched list of the "top 25" or the "top 50" something – banks, or insurance companies, or privately-held companies, manufacturing companies – whatever the topic for the week - in their area.

One list a week, throughout the year.

Each list contains top-level information about the company: name, address, phone, website, CEO, perhaps HR director, key clients (if they wish to provide that information), relevant sales statistics and other information that is both interesting and useful to your search for work.

All that valuable information, right there for you. Each *Business Journal* complies their lists into an annual publication called *The Book of Lists*. (See http://www.bizjournals.com/bookoflists/.)

The Book of Lists may be in book format, downloadable or on a disk. Check the website to see what's available.

When I have been in the job market, I found the *Book of Lists* to be a phenomenal resource. I cannot urge you strongly enough to purchase the *Book of Lists*, or better yet, to subscribe to the newspaper in the cities of your choice.

Be Bold: The Spaghetti or the Meatball?

💣* **A strong warning:** This strategy is for those of you who are working on your own.

*If you are working with a recruiter or executive search firm and they are submitting your credentials to a company, **under no circumstances** should you go around them and directly contact the company yourself.*

💣* **However,** if you are handling things on your own, with your new résumé in hand, and armed with an introduction to the top decision-makers found in *The Book of Lists* for the cities or regions of interest to you, you have the opportunity to take a bold step, moving from being spaghetti to becoming the meatball. Here's how:

💣* Consider acting boldly and sending your cover letter and functional résumé directly to the decision-makers found in **The Book of Lists.**

There is definitely risk in doing this. I know that.

Or you may look at it from this angle: You may be rewarded for your initiative, innovative thinking and the courage to stand out. You never know – the CEO may like what he or she sees and pass your résumé to HR for special attention. Or contact you directly. It happens. I know it happens. It happened to me.

♦* Be the meatball, not the spaghetti.

I know from years of personal experience that the HR department's primary function is to fill positions with the best-qualified people possible.

To do that, they strive to filter out the unqualified applicants while hopefully retaining the qualified ones.

Compounded by this difficult economy, staff cuts, computers and key-word searches, I also know that the process is definitely an imperfect one because it unfortunately filters out many well-qualified people who simply did not present themselves as effectively as their competitors.

It is not an intentional thing; it's just the way it is.

So it comes down to this: are you willing to be bold, to take a risk and step outside of the established process, or not?

To help you decide, let me tell you of a personal experience as a prelude to suggesting an alternative approach.

Some years ago, when the economy was in a slump, after only eight months on the job, I was one of 130 people who got laid off as my company downsized and my division disappeared. My position at the time was Divisional Vice President of Human Resources.

I received outplacement support, and for several months, I followed their guidelines. I did mass mailings like there was no tomorrow. I shot-gunned my résumé to lots of companies, going through the proper procedures and applying for specific positions as a Human Resources Vice President or HR Director.

I had been a Director for over ten years, and a VP for less than one year.

Several months into the search, I learned I was in a Catch-22. On one hand, I had not been a VP long enough to claim significant experience at that level. And on the other hand, a compassionate recruiter told me that folks trying to fill a Director-level position arbitrarily decided that since I had been a VP, I would not want to take a back-step to Director, and so they stepped back from me.

I spent a frustrating year watching my savings dribble away as I wedged myself again and again into the pack of applicants, all of us trying to squeeze in through HR's very narrow front door.

Following the traditional process, I sent out almost 300 résumés, locally and nationwide. I went on three interviews. I got no offers.

During one of those three interviews, the senior vice president of human resources semi-jokingly remarked that I was better qualified than he was and he figured his boss would replace him with me.

Catch-22 was alive and well.

When I came across the *Puget Sound Business Journal* and its corresponding *Book of Lists*, I had a flash of inspiration and I decided to be bold.

💣* I decided I no longer wanted to think of myself, or present myself, as a job applicant.

💣 I decided I'd had enough of being spaghetti; it was time to be the meatball.

💣 So, I put myself into the mindset of one professional asking another professional for assistance.

💣 If you're going to use this approach, I suggest you do the same.

💣 Using my functional résumé and two particular sets of words I am going to share with you, I sent my cover letter and résumé directly to the top people listed in several categories in the *Book of Lists* from the *Puget Sound Business Journal.*

I sent out 100 letters to CEOs, General Managers, Founders, Presidents and Managing Directors. In my cover letter, I said I was going to be in Seattle exploring job opportunities over a specific three-week time period and I asked for the opportunity to meet with them.

💣 ***GET THIS:*** *Twenty of those 100 people responded with appointments or invitations to visit when I got to Seattle.* A lot of them also made it a point to tell me they'd make sure I got a really good cup of coffee!

Can you believe it? *A 20 percent positive response!* I was using the same résumé, but a different cover letter, sent directly to the top.

💣 Four Magic Sentences for Your Cover Letter

After introducing myself, I opened the letter with these words:

"I am seeking referrals to people or companies where you think there might be a need for someone with my skills and experience. My résumé is attached."

Think about the first eight words of that first sentence.

I was not asking anyone for a job. I was asking for *referrals.*

I wanted a J-O-B. Why did I ask for *"referrals?"* What's the logic here?

Let's assume a couple of things: You are the decision-maker. You are a caring person, and your company is not presently in the market for an HR director.

If I tell you in my letter that I've been laid off and ask if you have a job for me and you do not, you'll tell me "no." And you'll probably feel some compassion for my situation and some regret having to say "no."

And it's likely that you may also feel some personal discomfort.

💣 To avoid feeling uncomfortable, you will probably take steps to actively and quickly distance yourself from me, the cause of your discomfort.

💣 In other words, if I ask you for a job and you have nothing for me, the conversation is over, right there.

💣 However, I was not asking for a job. I was asking for *"referrals."*

Now what's the logic?

💣* With just that little change, I am no longer an applicant (supplicant); I am more like a peer.

You are still that same caring decision-maker. If you like my résumé and you think it's possible I might be valuable somewhere, even if you don't have anything for me at the moment, there is a good chance that you'll be curious and will invite me in for coffee and conversation. And you may see something you like and end up making space and offering me a job, or not.

💣* **HOWEVER, and this is the critical point,** if you do *not* have work for me but like my cover letter and résumé, my request for *"referrals"* will have opened up an entirely different thought process in your mind.

Play it out in your mind and prove it to yourself. See if your thought process doesn't become narrow when you think, "I'm seeking a job" and expand when you think, "I'm seeking referrals."

Since people generally derive a warm feeling of happiness or pleasure when they can be helpful to someone needing assistance, or to a business colleague or friend, or stranger, the helpful thought process will likely continue.

I should tell you the results of my mailing:

I enjoyed a lot of great coffee during those 20 conversations, meetings and interviews.

I was given and followed up on a number of referrals

I ended up accepting a consulting assignment from one of the original 20 individuals and was relocated from back east to Vancouver, WA, where I remained for one year.

Before I finish up with the other set of critical words for the cover letter, let me give you another example of the benefit being the meatball, rather than the spaghetti.

When a company decided to do away with all of their field sales / marketing staff and go with distributor representatives, a number of people were let go, including a friend of mine and his boss.

I had the opportunity to create functional résumés for both of them.

My friend enthusiastically embraced the concept of his new functional résumé and applied his creativity to make it a truly personal and unique document.

His boss nit-picked me throughout the process and then nit-picked the end result. He nit-picked the nit-picks. He later redid his functional résumé into something that was neither reverse-chronological nor functional. I don't know how to describe it but the term "train wreck" comes to mind.

My friend's boss took his altered new résumé and began an intensive shotgun mailing campaign, sending the same document far and wide and using traditional channels.

💣 **My friend did not.** He used his time and energy to conduct a very focused campaign, *targeting only one company.* He knew where he wanted to work and knew with certainty they needed his marketing and sales expertise. *He knew he was the solution to the problem they had but did not know they had.*

💣 He analyzed their marketing practices, identified needs going unmet and created a unique marketing plan, just for them. He told them _what_ needed to be done, but _not how_ to do it. For the _how_ part, they needed to hire him.

Keeping his focus clearly on them and not on himself, he made sure they understood that, even if they did not hire him, his marketing plan was theirs to keep.

It took him two weeks of focused effort to create that plan. Working intermittently on his résumé, it took me about two days to blend his input and mine, then polish it to perfection.

When everything was ready, he completely bypassed the traditional HR channel and sent the plan, along with his new résumé and a targeted cover letter, to the senior vice president of marketing, and copied the CEO.

That was a very aggressive strategy and a gutsy move – sending his packet to his potential new boss, and to the boss's boss.

Remember my earlier comment that on one of my three interviews a VP of HR told me I was better qualified than he was and that his boss would likely replace him with me?

By sending a copy of his packet to the CEO, he gently but effectively made certain that, should he want to, the VP of Sales and Marketing would be unable to simply toss his information in the trash.

(If you want to learn more about that approach, take a look at Michael Boylan's creative book **The Power to Get In**.)

Three days after submitting his package, my friend met personally with both executives. By the end of the following week, he had negotiated his package and was on board.

Total time: one month from lay-off to starting his new position.

Four months later, I learned that his old boss was still flogging his hacked-up version of my functional résumé around the market.

Focusing on the company rather than on himself, my friend presented himself as the solution to a need going unmet, and he was snapped up in a New York Minute.

His boss? Who knows? We both lost track of him.

What will it be: meatball or spaghetti?

Now, let's wrap it up.

♠* In my experience, people who shotgun their résumés out to a large number of companies in hopes of generating some interest almost never think in terms of the needs of the potential employer, and mostly *never offer the potential employer anything of value at the outset.*

I believe that is a mistake.

My friend offered something valuable and significant - a marketing plan - whether or not they hired him.

♠* Earlier I said I changed my perspective *from* that of *job applicant asking for a job* to one *professional asking another professional for assistance.*

♠* Keeping that very different perspective in mind, here is the other set of important words, what I said in closing my letter to those 100 people.

♠* *"I view this as a request for assistance from one professional to another. I look forward to the opportunity to repay the favor."*

♠* Much as you need work, **your job search cannot, must not, be all about you.**

Professionals reciprocate favors. I chose to elevate myself to the level of one professional asking a favor of another, and in so doing I obligated myself to each of them. A few asked something of me in return and I reciprocated. Most did not and just went about their business, content to have been of service.

Four Magic Sentences

♠* While I cannot prove it, I believe that using these two sets of words:

"I am seeking referrals to people or companies where you think there might be a need for someone with my skills and experience. My résumé is attached."

AND

"I view this as a request for assistance from one professional to another. I look forward to the opportunity to repay the favor."

created a mindset in the recipients that helped set me apart from others in search of work.

I urge you to consider using **the twin concepts of *"seeking referrals"* *and* *"repaying the favor"*** as you proceed with your job search.

In Closing

I'm done and you're on your way.

This book has been about getting your phone to ring with a recruiter on the other end calling you in for an interview.

And further down the road, I'm planning three additional books to help you keep your career moving forward:

- *Social Networking with Your Functional Résumé,*
- *Interviews That Resume Careers, and*
- *The Accomplishments-Minded Employee.*

I wish you all the best possible success in your search.

Don@ResumesThatResumeCareers.com is my email address. I'd appreciate your feedback and suggestions for future editions of the book, and would love to hear how your search is going.

If you found the book helpful and would consider giving me a short testimonial for my website and future editions of my book, I'll say "thank you" with a special report, *"The Job Search From HR's Side of the Desk."*

Thank you very much, and my very best regards to you.

Don –

PS.   Once you have your completed first draft of your functional résumé in hand, you may decide you would like some editing and polishing help before sending it out.

If so, please go to www.ResumesThatResumeCareers.com and click on the "SERVICES" link.

a life can change in a tenth of
a second
or sometimes it can take
70
years.

\-   **Charles Bukowski**
you tell me what it means
The Flash of Lightening Behind the Mountain

Epilogue

Change.

Specifically, changing your behaviors and changing how you see yourself.

We have space for one more quick story.

For the first couple of decades of my life, I bit my fingernails. No, actually, I gnawed them to pretty much nothing.

One hot and sweaty summer day I was crawling around in the dirt out in the woods with my army unit. My scalp itched something fierce and I removed my helmet to really scratch my head. With no nails, all I got was an unsatisfactory fingertip rub.

I remember really looking at my fingertips and thinking how useless my nails were to me at that moment, and disgusting they looked, and how much I *really* wanted to *scratch* my head.

In that instant, I CHANGED. I realized I wasn't going to gnaw on them anymore.

That was over four decades ago.

SO WHAT?

So change can happen in a tenth of a second, or it can decades, or it can happen never.

Over the course of our time together, you've changed.

Please compare the résumé you were using before you read the book, and your new functional résumé.

Big change, I would imagine.

Please recall how you were feeling about your job search prospects then, and how you are feeling now.

Another big change, I think.

If you have really applied yourself to writing your accomplishments essays and then:

- distilled them to their essence in a very focused manner,
- thoughtfully identified your transferrable and motivated skills, and
- effectively compiled the rest of your résumé,

I am certain something you were not expecting has happened to you.

I believe your self-opinion, how you *really* see yourself, will have changed for the better.

If you began the book thinking, "I'm just a ......," I believe you have now discarded that notion forever and replaced it with this idea: "Damn, I'm good!

If you began the book thinking you had no accomplishments, I believe you have now discarded that opinion and have opened your eyes to the truth, and that truth is, "Damn, I'm good!"

If you began the book thinking there was no reason for you to have a functional résumé, I believe your self-awareness and self-worth has increased to the point that when you think of yourself, your first thought is, "Damn, I'm good!"

And if you began the book thinking that résumés based on accomplishments were only for managers and executives, I believe you have dropped that like the wrong idea it is, and have replaced it with, "Damn, I'm good! And I've got the résumé to prove it!"

(your) *"... life can change in a tenth of a second"*

I believe that at some point as you were reading the book, you had a little inkling. Something moved inside you, and *the real you* began to awaken, to emerge, as you changed.

You began to see yourself in a different light, see yourself as a different person.

Maybe you saw yourself as more capable.

Maybe you began to trust yourself more.

Maybe you felt an increase in your self-confidence.

Or perhaps you could actually "see" yourself doing the work you always thought was beyond you.

Or, maybe your subconscious grabbed on to the idea that you *ARE* the solution to some company's need that is going unmet

And you listened to your little voice inside you as it thundered out, "YES! I CAN!"

Whatever the change, please continue to blow gently on that little flame, feed it and nurture it until it grows into a bonfire that will consume all self-doubt and take you and your life where you want to go.

Good luck.

Not that you'll need it, because as you have discovered:

"DAMN! YOU'RE GOOD!"

Do you know job seekers
who need to read
Résumés That Resume Careers?

Please send them to
www.ResumesThatResumeCareers.com

For volume sales to corporations, libraries, government, or to assist our military to transition into civilian jobs, please go to:

www.ResumesThatResumeCareers.com/buybooks

For additional information, please call 800.597.9972

Advance Praise for
Résumés That Resume Careers

"Don Burrows doesn't miss a thing in this hot new book. It's about HOW TO stand out. This is functional profile methodology and its emphasis on customization and sharing your personal interests is right on in today's world dominated by social media. Don helps you uncover and present accomplishments that make you look like the rock star that you are. There are many great tips here for business people as well."

Mike O'Neil | President, Founder, Trainer, Speaker, Author, LinkedIn Rock Star
Author of *Rock The World with your Online Presence*.
LinkedIn Book
LinkedIn www.linkedin.com/in/mikeoneil 27,000+ connections
Twitter@mikeoneildenver 27,000+ followers

"Don's intelligent, insightful approach will help your résumé stand out and get you that interview."

JonScott Williams | Organization Development / Human Resources Consultant

"I have found his advice invaluable as I navigated my personal career journey. He is able to breathe confidence into the resume and into the candidate."

Rachel Braynin | Director, Global Support, ChannelAdvisors

Don Burrows. After three decades of helping individuals find work using *functional résumés,* Don brings that expertise to the world with the intention of helping thousands more get back to work. He and his wife live north of Seattle.

For updates and additional support, visit:
www.ResumesThatResumeCareers.com

Made in the USA
Charleston, SC
07 June 2010